STICKNEY-FOREST VIE'

3 1803 00128 8539

S0-AAE-148

Welcome to the EVERYTHING® series!

THESE HANDY, accessible books give you all you need to tackle a difficult project, gain a new hobby, comprehend a fascinating topic, prepare for an exam, or even brush up on something you learned back in school but have since forgotten.

You can read an *EVERYTHING®* book from cover-to-cover or just pick out the information you want from our four useful boxes: e-facts, e-ssentials, e-alerts, and e-questions. We literally give you everything you need to know on the subject, but throw in a lot of fun stuff along the way, too.

We now have well over 150 *EVERYTHING®* books in print, spanning such wide-ranging topics as weddings, pregnancy, wine, learning guitar, one-pot cooking, managing people, and so much more. When you're done reading them all, you can finally say you know *EVERYTHING®*!

 **FACTS:** Important sound bytes of information

 **ESSENTIALS:** Quick and handy tips

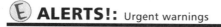 **ALERTS!:** Urgent warnings

 **QUESTIONS:** Solutions to common problems

THE
EVERYTHING®
Series

Dear Reader:

I recently found this quote from the illustrious financial wizard J. P. Morgan: "Millionaires don't use astrology. Billionaires do." Hah! I thought. Funny . . . and true! We've used the planets and the stars as our guide since the fourth century B.C. Why? Because they influence everything we do in life—from health to luck to love.

Just ask Johannes Kepler, Isaac Newton, or Louis Pasteur.

I'm always surprised when people ask me if astrology is real. Predictably, their skepticism has to do with an averseness to the generalizations that have plagued astrology since the beginning: Virgo is finicky; Leo is arrogant; Sagittarius has wanderlust. Where is the three-dimensional person? Where is the beauty of the individual? In truth, claims such as these are stereotypical, at best, and inaccurate, at worst.

I'm from New York, but I live in Italy. People sigh when I tell them about my home in Tuscany and my real-life fairy-tale romance. I say: Anyone can have what I have. You just have to know where to look. Here. Read up and find out. Your future awaits.

Warm wishes from me,

Jenni Kosarin

THE
EVERYTHING®
LOVE
SIGNS
BOOK

Use astrology to find your perfect mate!

Jenni Kosarin

Adams Media
Avon, Massachusetts

For Daniel, my love.

Copyright ©2004, F+W Publications, Inc.
All rights reserved. This book, or parts thereof, may not be reproduced
in any form without permission from the publisher; exceptions
are made for brief excerpts used in published reviews.

An Everything® Series Book.
Everything® and everything.com® are registered trademarks
of F+W Publications, Inc.

Published by Adams Media, an F+W Publications Company
57 Littlefield Street, Avon, MA 02322 U.S.A.
www.adamsmedia.com

ISBN: 1-59337-040-7
Printed in Canada.

J I H G F E D C B

Library of Congress Cataloging-in-Publication Data
Kosarin, Jenni.
The everything love signs book / Jenni Kosarin.
p.   cm.   •
(An everything series book)
ISBN 1-59337-040-7
1. Astrology. 2. Love–Miscellanea. 3. Mate selection—Miscellanea.
4. Sex–Miscellanea. I. Title. II. Series: Everything series.
BF1729.L6K67 2004
133.5'864677—dc22
2003021468

This publication is designed to provide accurate and authoritative information
with regard to the subject matter covered. It is sold with the understanding that
the publisher is not engaged in rendering legal, accounting, or other professional
advice. If legal advice or other expert assistance is required, the services of a
competent professional person should be sought.
—From a *Declaration of Principles* jointly adopted by a
Committee of the American Bar Association and
a Committee of Publishers and Associations

Many of the designations used by manufacturers and sellers to distinguish their
products are claimed as trademarks. Where those designations appear in this
book and Adams Media was aware of a trademark claim, the designations have
been printed with initial capital letters.

Illustrations by Barry Littmann.

*This book is available at quantity discounts for bulk purchases.
For information, call 1-800-872-5627.*

Visit the entire Everything® series at everything.com

THE

EVERYTHING
Series

EDITORIAL

Publishing Director: Gary M. Krebs
Managing Editor: Kate McBride
Copy Chief: Laura MacLaughlin
Acquisitions Editor: Bethany Brown
Development Editor: Patrycja Pasek-Gradziuk
Production Editor: Jamie Wielgus

PRODUCTION

Production Director: Susan Beale
Production Manager: Michelle Roy Kelly
Series Designer: Daria Perreault
Cover Design: Paul Beatrice and Frank Rivera
Layout and Graphics: Colleen Cunningham,
Rachael Eiben, Michelle Roy Kelly,
Daria Perreault, Erin Ring

☆ *Contents* ☆

ACKNOWLEDGMENTS xi
TOP TEN LOVE SIGN COUPLES xii
INTRODUCTION xiii

CHAPTER 1 *Aries* 1
The Aggressor. 2
A Power Play 6
The Art of Attraction. 7
Pillow Talk: Signs in the Bedroom. 11
Sun Love Matches 15
Love Planets: Venus and Mercury 24

CHAPTER 2 *Taurus* 27
The Conqueror 28
You Can't Hurry Love 30
The Art of Attraction 31
Pillow Talk: Signs in the Bedroom. 35
Sun Love Matches 40
Love Planets: Venus and Mercury 47

CHAPTER 3 *Gemini*. 49

The Born Storyteller 50

Split Personality 52

The Art of Attraction 54

Pillow Talk: Signs in the Bedroom. 57

Sun Love Matches 61

Love Planets: Venus and Mercury 69

CHAPTER 4 *Cancer*. 71

The Expansive Heart 72

A Fine Romance 74

The Art of Attraction 76

Pillow Talk: Signs in the Bedroom. 78

Sun Love Matches 81

Love Planets: Venus and Mercury 89

CHAPTER 5 *Leo* 91

The Generous Lion. 92

Queenly/Kingly Behavior 93

The Art of Attraction 94

Pillow Talk: Signs in the Bedroom. 97

Sun Love Matches. 100

Love Planets: Venus and Mercury 109

CHAPTER 6 *Virgo* 111

The Selective One. 112

A Battle Within. 113

The Art of Attraction 114

Pillow Talk: Signs in the Bedroom 117

Sun Love Matches. 118

Love Planets: Venus and Mercury 127

CHAPTER 7 *Libra* **129**
Libra, the Fair 130
Eye of the Storm 132
The Art of Attraction 133
Pillow Talk: Signs in the Bedroom 135
Sun Love Matches. 138
Love Planets: Venus and Mercury 144

CHAPTER 8 *Scorpio* **147**
The Dark One 148
You're Mine 150
The Art of Attraction 151
Pillow Talk: Signs in the Bedroom 154
Sun Love Matches. 156
Love Planets: Venus and Mercury 164

CHAPTER 9 *Sagittarius* **167**
The Renaissance Man (or Woman) 168
R-E-S-P-E-C-T 169
The Art of Attraction 170
Pillow Talk: Signs in the Bedroom 173
Sun Love Matches. 176
Love Planets: Venus and Mercury 183

CHAPTER 10 *Capricorn* **187**
The Strong, Silent One 188
Emotional Power. 190
The Art of Attraction 192
Pillow Talk: Signs in the Bedroom 195
Sun Love Matches. 197
Love Planets: Venus and Mercury 205

CHAPTER 11 *Aquarius* 207

The Eclectic 208

Higher Beings. 209

The Art of Attraction 210

Pillow Talk: Signs in the Bedroom. 212

Sun Love Matches. 215

Love Planets: Venus and Mercury 223

CHAPTER 12 *Pisces*. 225

The Sage 226

Savvy and Sassy. 227

The Art of Attraction 228

Pillow Talk: Signs in the Bedroom. 230

Sun Love Matches. 233

Love Planets: Venus and Mercury 241

Appendix A: ADDITIONAL RESOURCES 243
Appendix B: QUICK SUN SIGN CHART 244
Appendix C: VENUS: LOVE SIGN; MERCURY:
COMMUNICATION AND
INTELLIGENCE 245

INDEX. 267

Acknowledgments

Love to Paul and Donna Kosarin (Sagittarius and Pisces, respectively) . . . superb editors—you two missed your calling. Your genuine and generous spirit, continually romantic even after forty-five (plus) years, sets the bar for all potential soul mates. You have inspired me as well as all those around you with the true love you have. Thank you for everything you are and everything you've done.

My deepest thanks go to (Virgo) acquisitions editor Bethany Brown for her constant support and guidance—it's obvious that you love these projects as much as I do! Thanks also to Melissa DuShane (Capricorn) for being brilliant . . . I know it just comes naturally to you. And to Laura MacLaughlin (Leo) for going the extra distance.

Thank you all!

Top Ten Love Sign Couples

1. **Pisces woman/Sagittarius man:** Who says Fire and Water clash? This couple sizzles!

2. **Aries woman/Aries man:** Rocket launchers and firecrackers. You can't beat these two.

3. **Taurus woman/Aquarius man:** You won't find a stranger couple—they're odd together, but it seems to work.

4. **Cancer woman/Scorpio man:** If she can overlook his political views and deal with the stress that comes from his work, they're a match made in heaven.

5. **Leo woman/Aries man:** Thank goodness Aries is a real man, the Lioness thinks. She also loves the fact that people look up to him.

6. **Virgo woman/Scorpio man:** Both like to analyze, and they get along wonderfully.

7. **Aquarius woman/Taurus man:** Taurus is sensuous and daring; she's intrigued by his down-to-earth approach to life.

8. **Capricorn woman/Libra man:** Libra brings out Capricorn's happy side, and Capricorn gives Libra the kind of emotional security he's looking for.

9. **Libra woman/Aquarius man:** Who would've thought? Somehow, though, they truly balance each other out.

10. **Scorpio woman/Scorpio man:** These two go together so well that it's a little scary.

☆ *Introduction* ☆

"Courteous reader, Astrology is one of the most ancient sciences, held in high esteem of old, by the Wise and the Great. Formerly, no Prince would make war or peace; nor any General fight in battle. In short, no important affair was undertaken without first consulting an astrologer."

—Benjamin Franklin (1706–1790), signer of Declaration of Independence; scientist, printer, economist, philosopher

Heartbreak. A love gone wrong. A whirlwind romance and then a big breakup. These sound pretty much like the basic themes of your typical bad country song. (They may well be.) But they're also moments justifiably crooned about—unfortunate, albeit necessary parts of life. And they happen without warning, without reason . . . and sometimes, as luck would have it, without an essential neverending stock of double-fudge chocolate chunk ice cream.

Really, love sometimes feels like an affliction that's forced on you in an instant, without your control: Achoo! And then it's gone as quickly as it came.

Now what if someone could clue you in to the mysteries and secrets of your "other half" before you became irrevocably involved? What if someone could give you sound advice before the bedlam and the bother, the inevitable heartache? Even better, what if you could know exactly what you're looking for in a perfect mate and know who may be right or wrong for you even before the first date? It sounds impossible, doesn't it?

It's not; it's real. It's called love astrology. And you could learn it all from one comprehensive book—*The Everything® Love Signs Book*—the key to discovering your future before it happens. From the information gathered here, you'll get a glimpse of the future, what to expect from a potential life partner, and what an astrological soul mate really is. You'll understand your other half's likes and dislikes on all fronts: financial, emotional, spiritual, intellectual, and sexual. In other words, you'll discover everything essential for personally assessing the true possibilities of your future together.

Above all, you should always remember that nothing is set in stone. There are always ways to overcome obstacles and handicaps. If you find the man or woman of your dreams, don't rule that person out! Instead, read everything there is to know about him or her here. Then go about making future plans accordingly. Love-sign astrology exists to help you, not hinder you. Arm yourself before the battle, and you'll always come out ahead.

In short, life is complex; people are complex. Astrology is not. It can be learned. Sun-sign matches are one way to predict love compatibility—but they're not enough. Your Venus, for example, is your love sign—a spiritual beacon. A compatible sign in Mercury indicates a meeting of the minds. This one book brings all of these themes together, with easy-to-read charts in the back—all accessible, with a birth date and an interest.

There are also essential (fun! naughty!) sexual tips that will work before *and* during intimacy, and seduction techniques based on astrological clues.

In effect, love can be a scary subject and so can handing your heart out on a silver platter. But love astrology is simple. If you absorb the necessary information here, one can easily be applied to the other. Because once you combine the two, you have the relationship advantage.

And that's nothing to sneeze at.

Chapter 1
Aries

Let's talk about the Ram. Powerful, charismatic, and a real star, Aries is the first sign of the zodiac and quite a charmer, too, in love and romance. Some of the stereotypes associated with the Aries personality are true, and some aren't. Let's have a look at a more three-dimensional Aries. Here we put the pieces together and finally make sense of it all.

The Aggressor

It's true. Aries is aggressive. But more specifically, Aries is a go-getter. In romance or business, Aries always aims to come out on top. He's instinctive and a great negotiator, with a natural gift of organizing things like conferences or interviews. People gravitate toward him because he's never boring. Unfortunately, many Aries never quite get to the point where they're actually happy with their work. Somehow this always affects their love situations. In truth, it's never really about the money, though that's always a nice incentive. Instead, it has more to do with recognition and status. Yes, work is very important to Aries—man or woman. And there's a very good reason for this.

Aries are the children of the zodiac. However mature an Aries is, she will want something not quite within her reach—not unlike a child who has had a rubber ducky taken from her in the bathtub. Unfortunately, this affects her way of dealing with romance. When she's not content with her work life, there is nothing a partner can do to make her happy. She can become moody and lose her enchanting sense of humor. When this happens, watch out! Aries can be as crabby as Cancer or Scorpio.

The Perceptive Eye

There is one difference, though, from the other, less fixed signs: Aries is practical about his options. He intuitively knows what he can and cannot have and what he's capable of achieving. Therefore, Aries will attack a problem—whether in love or business—at full force but with a discerning eye. He does this because if he doesn't conquer and win, his ego will have a hard time of it. He can rush head-on into any romantic or business situation, becoming unduly wowed by his partner or prospect. But know this—Aries will eventually catch on; grasping the situation completely in definitive terms, good or bad. If it's the latter, he'll be out the door without a second glance.

 ALERT!

> Aries will never methodically search out advice. When it comes to a tough situation, she'll take others' ideas and apply them to the situation at hand, calling them her own. But beware! If you call her on it, she may just get defensive and turn everything around on you.

At his best, Aries is romantic, exciting, and exceptionally fun to be with. Though he's more inclined to pounce on a grand romance and then pull back in an instant, he does make a loyal partner in the long run—in his own way. True, Aries is not the most faithful sign of the zodiac, though he expects you to be. But he does esteem and cherish any significant other with whom he chooses to spend his time.

Seeking Perfection

Another thing not highly known about Aries men and women is that they're seriously idealistic. Though Aries is pragmatic with goals, she wants more than anything to achieve greatness. This, too, filters into home life. When it comes to love and family, Aries will look for her ideal partner—though chances are that she won't find him early in the game. But Aries is not critical and judgmental, like Taurus or Scorpio. She'll throw a choice comment this way or that once in awhile but, in truth, Aries is too wrapped up in what she's doing to see clearly what's going on around her. She expects her significant other to be perfect, too, and without her guidance.

 FACT

A contradiction in terms, Aries wants an easy-going partner—but also needs a good chase. A perfect love match for Aries is someone who is neither high-maintenance nor a pushover. This is a tricky blend but one that is worthy of the typical Aries' affections.

Strangely enough, Aries is the least-guilty sign of the zodiac. Like a child, Aries is convinced of his innocence, believing that if he messes up (or cheats!) it's warranted—at least in his case. Don't bother reminding Aries you were right. He's already mentally reshaped events to accommodate his take of the situation. To Aries, it's his way or the highway.

Don't try fawning all over Aries, telling her she's fascinating. She knows it already, and she'll start to think, "That's right. I am fascinating. In fact, I'm probably too good for you." Aries doesn't want excessive compliments. Instead, she wants to earn your affections. But she'll never leave a good thing. After all, the object of the game is to find the one you can trust and love forever, right? Aries is aware of this and will try all avenues before settling down for good.

Though family is very important to him, many Aries have considerable difficulty with estranged brothers or sisters or critical parents. This is one of the reasons that he'll search for the ultimate partner. Sometimes Aries even gets engaged not just once but two or three times. When he's signed the contract, though, you'll most likely have won an Aries forever. It's not easy to get him to the altar. Once accomplished, it's probably a union that will last.

 ESSENTIAL

> Fortunately, Aries will not dawdle with ideas. If there's something he doesn't like, he'll tell you right away. Aries expects you to listen and take notice. It's not a warning—it's more of a command.

A Power Play

If you've ever been involved with an Aries for a long period, at some point you've no doubt come to a standstill in the relationship. Aries is inexplicably drawn to situations that require a bigger scheme. This means that his undeniable wisdom will eventually enter into the picture. He needs to feel useful and to apply his incredible wisdom to make everything "right." Aries is probably convinced that his way is the best way. If he's challenged too often, he'll give a few telltale signs that he's had enough. Then he'll just walk away, without warning. Though he may place the occasional ego call to determine whether or not the significant other is still interested, he doesn't necessarily care what the answer is either way. Once he's made up his mind, that's it. When this happens, it's a sure sign the relationship is over.

 QUESTION?

Can a fling with an Aries turn into something more?
Probably not. You'll have to start with good behavior from the very beginning. Aries rates her partners. She wants a perfect mate, not just a play buddy.

Aries likes to be in control of things—but she'll despise you if you can't stand up to her in a way she deems worthy of her respect. Call it power, call it power play, Aries will not be manipulated to do another's bidding, though she'll still want her man to be strong. She'll also want someone who's calm and cool but who can effortlessly keep up with her adventures without stifling her—it's a tall order for Aries woman, but one she requires to keep the boredom at bay.

"Give Me Freedom, Or . . ."

Power does have a key influence in the Aries relationship, though it affects this sign in a rather odd way. All Aries are independent and need a lot of space. Even though he loves affection, sincerity, and unconditional love from a partner he prizes, Aries still wants the freedom to go out or stay in when he feels like it. This is a very delicate balance to achieve. No one can hold an Aries down—and no one should. The one true way to maintain a person of this sign is to let him do what he wants to do. Give him space and freedom. If he's truly the one for you, he'll be back. Aries hates to be proved wrong. If he's invested time and money into any effort (including a relationship), he won't be so quick to watch it fizzle out before his eyes.

The Art of Attraction

It's stupid to play games in love, right? Wrong. Aries will almost never go for the easy target. For Aries, man or woman, the chase is essential and lends to the excitement. In fact, add a sense of "hope we don't get caught," and you've found yourself a winning plan.

Granted, this will only work for the beginning period of the courtship. Read on to determine what will keep an Aries by your side.

The Long Haul

Sure, Aries seems jealous and possessive. He is, to a point—though not to the degree of Scorpio, Cancer, or even Virgo. Truthfully, Aries simply cannot imagine someone would actually leave him for another . . . and he's usually right. He's sexy and charming—dashing, even. With Aries, jealousy is almost a test, as in, "Let's see how much my partner loves me." And with that answer, he'll be free to go back to more important tasks—typically related to career and work.

 ESSENTIAL

Aries wants a stable partner; one who's emotionally balanced and independent. Aries will also control the situation by seeking out security. If you're faithful and know how to stand up to Aries, you've got a mate for life.

Aries is also always quite sure of himself and of the situation at hand, even if the cockiness is not warranted. There's a reason for this, too. Aries craves security. She seeks it out. While a Capricorn gives a sense of stability, Aries is strangely drawn to it. She won't put herself in a position that's not 150 percent solid. It's okay for an

Aries to stray, but if she thinks her partner is unfaithful (or intends to cheat), she won't hesitate to move on.

Speaking of independence, Aries needs to know that you have your own life, your own friends, career, and outside interests. Aries distrusts clingers and doesn't want an overly jealous mate (though some jealousy helps him feel secure). If you're out of work, don't stay that way for long. Aries won't tolerate it.

Here's another secret about the Ram—he's a social beast. If not for any other reason, Aries likes to be out there, ready to butt heads with others, ready to defend his cause. He needs to be noticed and recognized for his cool savvy, his sharp business sense, and for his charm. Aries is almost never a nerd. He's always on the lookout for contacts, whether professional or personal. Aries will also go in spurts, partying regularly and then staying home for periods of time. If you want to keep Aries, let him do what he needs to do. Live your life, and make room for him in it. He'll push his way back when he's ready.

He/She: The Little Stuff Counts

Like other Fire signs, Aries loves to be worshipped. Unlike Leo, who tends to be more modest about it, Aries puts it out there, letting you build up her ego as much as you can. She deserves it, she believes, after all. Insult Aries in a hard-nosed or vulgar way, and you'll be heading in the wrong direction. Present an issue to Aries delicately, on a politically correct platter, and you'll earn the respect of any Aries, male or female.

Aries' Style

Aries people have a particular fashion sense, and it's usually not conservative. Styles range from funky to slick to mod and even weird. They'll expect you to have one of your own. They want a mate to look good on their arm. That said, Aries women, for instance, like distinguished-looking men. Though she herself may have a colorful style, she often likes a man who dresses in a conventional way. Aries men, on the other hand, admire a woman who can look feminine and still look sexy with bold garments, like leather pants and a jacket with a low-cut silk top.

 FACT

> Aries is practical when it comes to finding a love partner. He also leans toward the tidy side of the spectrum. If a would-be mate of Aries man ever left lipstick on the pillowcase, for example, it would be the quick cause of a no-nonsense dismissal.

All in all, Aries tends to be a little selfish. You may want to look elsewhere for a compliment, though subtle flattery works on Aries, himself. If you want to know how you look, ask someone else. You'll just get a "good" or "fine" mumbled on his way out. On top of that, Aries can be turned off by unsure or wishy-washy comportment.

In short, Aries likes a mate with bold moves. She likes to be surprised. Show her to a place she's never heard of, spend a little money, and be outrageous. Too much mystery will not cause Aries to stall. She'll follow you to the ends of the earth to conquer you. Don't let her—at least, not right away.

The Sex Issue

. . . Which leads us to the topic of sex. Aries has a hearty appetite for it and is also quite good at the sport. He'll expect you to know your way around the bedroom, too—though he may have to convince himself first that it's more than just another roll in the hay. Press too hard or pressure to move ahead too quickly, and Aries will beat a hasty retreat to the door. Because he's intuitive, he'll happily let you manipulate him with sex, but only if and when it's his will at the moment. Aries eventually thinks ahead to the long-term, though, even if his attentions waver at any given moment. So find a good balance with this exciting, unpredictable creature, and do read on.

Pillow Talk: Signs in the Bedroom

The key to keeping a sex life spiced up with the Ram includes providing satisfaction in every way but always keeping a little enticement waiting. If you bore Aries, in or out of the bedroom, the skid marks she's left won't be the only sign she's not coming back. Try telling her you have a secret sexual maneuver that you'll just have to show her later. She'll do her best to get you back into bed. And remember, Aries likes to at least *think* she's in control at all times, even in the most intimate and compromising of positions.

The Secret Aries Man

What to do with a male Ram? You've got your work cut out for you. Aries men mostly prefer rough and tough over slow and sultry—they just don't have the patience. But they can hold out. So, if you're the type who likes a man to take charge and dominate you in bed, here's your guy.

He may be interested in knowing what makes you tick and what you like. Tell him, but do it with grace. You can compliment him first on what a fabulous lover he is, then suggest or hint at things you like, letting him believe that it was really his idea in the first place. Aries will take your cue and excel at whatever task you place in front of him. In fact, he'll love the idea of any good challenge.

The Aries Lover

Unfortunately, the typical Aries man can be ego-centric in bed, too. But that's okay. There's one way to remedy this: Put an end to it immediately. In other words, don't wait a year to let this problem slip out in a verbal fight. (Aries will be devastated by the mere hint that he's been doing something wrong in the sack—though at the same time he probably won't believe it.) The truth is, Aries man may be more wrapped up in his own needs, but he'll be more than happy to meet yours, too. He just has to understand what those requirements are, and that means you have to clue him in. He's not a bad lover. It's more that, at times, he's an oblivious one.

 ALERT!

> Strangely enough, Aries man will be up front about what he doesn't like . . . but he doesn't want you to be! Aries is sensitive; he has thin skin. If you reprimand him, do it gently.

Bedroom Play

When it comes to bedroom play, Aries likes to try everything once. If he hints or talks outright about trying a little ménage-a-trois, chances are he plans on doing it anyway, with or without you. Aries men take their own words seriously. He might tell you it's getting late, and you'd better get home now or he'll be too tired to make love. If he says it, it's a sure bet he means it. He won't go back on his word. Aries men should be believed when they say something, in bed or otherwise. Heed the warning, and adjust accordingly. Are you ready for the male Ram?

The Secret Aries Woman

Like her male counterpart, the female Ram loves to get attention but needs a good challenge. Compliment her excessively and you're making a mistake. She'll like you and enjoy your company, but she'll never go to bed with you. Don't be her personal throw rug. She'll walk all over you and leave you out to dry. She wants a strong man—one who will stand up to her but who will allow her to take the lead.

Note that there's a difference here between *allowing* her to and *letting* her do what she wants. An Aries woman will know when you're controlling her. If you're "allowing" her, she'll respect you more and believe you've got power. If you're "letting" her get away with things, she'll push the envelope further, thinking you're too weak to keep her. Then she'll go looking for another man worthy of her affections.

 ALERT!

Even though you should never go overboard with an Aries woman, if she's lacking the attention and ego-soothing words she expects from you, she will look elsewhere. Keep on your toes to please a Ram. Balance is the key, always leaving a little secrecy at the end.

Bedroom Escapades

Here's the rub. Like other Fire signs, Aries will expect her man to be superhuman in the bedroom. Outside, she wants to be the dominant force. In bed, though, she wants her man to take the lead. Though she believes herself to be in total control at all times, she surreptitiously wishes for an experience that will make the earth shake, causing her to lose it.

Like the Aries man, an Aries woman is a little wild and is curious enough to try out all new sexual adventures, positions, and exploits. A soft, slow, sweet lovemaking session will only irk an Aries woman—she'll be left with something similar to a metaphorical itch. She'll want to scratch it. And that, of course, will leave you in the dust.

Keeping the Excitement

She'll look for a man who's not googly-eyed over her. An Aries woman wants to respect and look up to you as a real he-man. In fact, telling an Aries woman that you love her (too soon) is a sure way to get her out the door. Chances are, she won't be back. This woman is all burning passion and fire, and she needs the same in a sexual mate. The key here is to always keep things exciting. One thing is for sure: She'll do the same for you.

Sun Love Matches

The typical Aries woman has more tact than Aries man. Though she can be brutally honest, she's a little better at holding back criticism than her male counterpart. Because of this, she can get along with more signs than the Aries man. But the Aries woman is more selective. Both genders fall in love quickly and then sometimes realize they've made a grave mistake, though the Aries woman is more difficult to win over. Plus, an Aries woman won't tolerate a man dominating her, while an Aries man will just become amused with the notion. Let's break that down. Below are the different possible pairings for an Aries woman, the femme fatale.

Aries Man

Think rocket launchers and firecrackers. These two, when teamed up, are a force not to be beat. Turn them against one another, though, and they're likely to verbally fight to the end. Aries man excites Aries woman. There's no other man in the zodiac who can make her feel important the way he can. It's love at first sight, too, with great chemistry in and out of the bedroom. Unfortunately, both signs are impatient and restless—and both need a lot of security. Thankfully, Aries man is willing to take a back seat to Aries woman's antics. If they can be delicate with each other's feelings and give each other plenty of space without becoming too emotionally distant, this can be a good long-term affair—and a probable chance for marriage.

 FACT

Just to get an idea of how sexy an Aries man actually is, think dashing: Sir Alec Guinness, Warren Beatty, James Caan, Andy Garcia, Robert Downey, Jr., Timothy Dalton (James Bond even!), and Marlon Brando. Oh, and let's not forget Casanova, himself.

Taurus Man

True to his Bull sign, Taurus man is stubborn. So is Aries woman. A Taurus man can sometimes get a little too clingy and possessive for Aries (and even obsessive at times), but his bedroom prowess will impress her off the charts. She also loves to be wined and dined by the Bull, though it may sometimes annoy her that he's only conditionally generous. In other words, he wants something for his efforts, and Aries won't put up with it: Aries woman wants to go with the flow. Also, she'll provoke and frustrate Taurus to the limit . . . even if he'll only fall more in love with her for it. If she can stay still long enough for Taurus to win her, this can be a good partnership. The potential is great for a passionate affair and perhaps marriage.

 ALERT!

The typical Taurus man likes going slow; Aries woman is in a rush to get where she's going. If she goes too fast (especially to bed), Taurus man will run the other way! He wants to get to know her—at his own leisurely pace. Aries woman needs to have a little patience with the romantic Bull.

Gemini Man

A Gemini man is likely to win over an Aries woman right from the get-go. But even if Gemini is charming, attractive, and interesting to Aries, he may not be grounded enough to keep her. His antics will wear on her patience quickly—what little there is of it—and the love affair may end. A Gemini man in bed, though, may have the kind of erotic sensuality and sustenance an Aries woman needs. His games will intrigue her, though he'll tend not to follow through—which may disappoint Aries. She's off in one direction, and he's off in the other, making these two a difficult love relationship to sustain. Though it's a quirky combination, Aries woman/Gemini man can have a good affair and possibly a long-term relationship.

Cancer Man

Believe it or not, these two together can be a successful couple. They're so different—like night and day. But Cancer man has found his match in fire and passion. Aries woman has it in bucketfuls. In fact, a Cancer man will be intrigued by an Aries woman and will want to know her secrets right away. If he's patient and doesn't push too hard, he'll eventually discover them.

 FACT

Cancer men have substance to them—they're strong and complex—and they'll want a mate who's emotionally deep, too. Tom Cruise, Harrison Ford, Tom Hanks, John Cusack, Dan Aykroyd, and Sylvester Stallone are all well-known Cancer men.

His calmness inspires Aries to sit down and take a break. If Cancer man is willing to wait at home while Aries parties, or will let her at least get into the spotlight once in awhile, this can be a good match. Sexually, the two are soul mates. This is a great long-term affair, with marriage a possibility.

Leo Man

Leo man loves to strut his stuff, and this impresses Aries. Leo, too, will be unduly awed by her directness. He'll also be proud to carry a sexy Aries woman on his arm.

 ALERT!

> Leo man is typically more faithful than the sly Aries woman. If she's got someone else on the side, instinctive Leo man will sense it immediately. He'll either push her away or find someone else, too—his fierce pride simply won't tolerate the betrayal.

Unfortunately, the Leo man likes to be boss—and so does the Aries woman. In the bedroom, Leo's got the moves Aries has waited for. But he may be a little shocked when he's in the mood for some affection and Aries is halfway out the door. Leo is also more sensitive than Aries, though both egos need to be pumped up endlessly. Passion-wise, the two are well matched.

This union is a possible long-term affair and even has the potential for marriage, though it's not probable.

Virgo Man

Virgo man is incredibly goal-oriented, and so is Aries woman. While Aries is good at getting the ball rolling, Virgo won't stop until the task is done and done well. Virgo is great at managing Aries' affairs, but he'll be convinced she's not handling things correctly—namely, the way he would do it. In addition, Aries jumps from subject to subject while Virgo is more curious and thorough. This will irritate Virgo man, who will feel like he's playing mental Ping-Pong (though this may actually make him desire her more—she's a puzzle he's dying to piece together). In bed, Aries woman will be impressed by Virgo's attentiveness and passion. Virgo man will undoubtedly be attracted to Aries woman's Fire, though he's not sure if he can control it—and he wants to. This worries him. Though he'll try to analyze her, Aries will beg him to stop. Although this is a possible long-term relationship, it's not a probable marriage.

Libra Man

Libra man is a poet. Aries woman is wowed by this. Unfortunately, when Aries woman realizes that his Libra Fire is more hypothetical, she may go off looking for someone who can love her with more conviction. In and out of the bedroom, Libra is sexy, sensual, and charismatic. Aries is definitely attracted to him. But Libra loves to keep his cool, and if there's one woman who can make him lose it, it's Aries woman. In fact, Libra thinks Aries is a bit bossy. Though he'd love to take the risk, he'll most likely back off and look for easier prey. In bed, though, these two make erotic sex look tame—together, they can take pleasure to new heights. If Libra takes a chance on Aries, the two could make a good long-term relationship, with marriage possible.

Scorpio Man

Speaking of great sex, Scorpio man and Aries woman can hole up for weeks on end and never see daylight. In bed, these two rock. Unfortunately, Scorpio's moodiness will affect Aries natural playfulness, and the fighting will start. Both are players. Scorpio is notoriously possessive, but Aries will take it more from her dark mate than she would from Cancer or Virgo.

 QUESTION?

Who's got the bigger temper?
Scorpio man does, of course. He's the only one (besides Aries man) who can match Aries woman's fury beat for beat. Unfortunately, Scorpio man is more underhanded than Aries woman. She may have a tough time figuring out her Scorpio man's manipulative verbal strategies.

Aries woman will be curious about Scorpio's well-hidden secrets, but if she suspects that she can't trust him, she won't think twice about looking elsewhere for solid ground. Scorpio is more complex and can sometimes drag Aries woman down with his "I've-got-the-weight-of-the-world-on-my-shoulders" attitude. If they find a good balance, and if Aries can leave Scorpio alone when he's stressed and feeling sorry for himself, this can be a good couple, with long-term relationship and even marriage potential.

Sagittarius Man

These two can be great together. If there's one man in the zodiac who won't bore Aries woman, it's definitely Sagittarius man. He'll even let her lead, though she knows he can take the helm if need be. And he's the he-man she's looking for—both in and out of bed. In fact, sex between these two can get out of hand. It's wild, naughty, and exciting. There is one problem, though. Sagittarius man has absolutely no tact. He says it straight. While Aries woman admires this, she also tires of it and wishes her nearly perfect other half would learn to keep his mouth shut once in awhile! Both are charming, sexy, and fun. This is a great love match, with good odds for marriage.

Capricorn Man

These two together are like children in a candy shop. They're two of the three innocents of the zodiac (with Leo being the other), and they see things with optimism and wonder. They love to laugh and joke, twenty-four hours a day, seven days a week. Though it is said that Capricorn man usually provides security to his mate, he finds a tough time with Aries woman. She wants to take the lead often, and this makes him turn the other way. Both signs have a difficult time committing but, if they do, they go well together. In the bedroom, Aries likes Capricorn's straight-to-it style, but she wouldn't mind getting down and dirty, too. Though Capricorn would like nothing better, he'll never admit it. So the two might wind up having "polite" sex, all the while hoping they can find a better bed plan. But shortcomings are superficial. These two have a good shot at something long-term, with marriage possible.

Aquarius Man

Aquarius man is more detached and sometimes even more superficial than Aries woman. What an odd feeling for Aries! In fact, he's even more unpredictable than she is—though this will inevitably turn her on and make her want Aquarius man more. In truth, she's envious of the Aquarius lifestyle and his take-it-or-leave-it approach. His strangeness intrigues her, while his bold approach to life makes her feel she's found her soul match. In bed, the two get restless easily and search for ways together to relieve the boredom. Aries, though, is more fiery. Aquarius man is more interested in performance than Aries woman's lose-yourself-in-the-moment sex style. In the end, these two can have an interesting love match and a possible marriage.

ESSENTIAL

Aquarius men are popular—everybody loves them. In fact, they're always in the limelight, even if they don't necessarily choose to be. This irks Aries woman. She'll want a little attention, too. If Aquarius man is willing to let her have it, these two can be good together.

Pisces Man

The Pisces man is utterly enthralled by Aries woman. He won't know what to do with her or how to handle her—she's a complete enigma to him. This is a shame because he has the power to control Aries woman with his passion and sensitivity—he's deep enough to keep Aries woman curious. He's also worldly, like she is. And he's a powerful soul, both romantic and expressive. Though Aries woman's first wish will be to unravel the mysterious Pisces man, she may get quickly frustrated by Pisces' beat-around-the-bush strategy and look elsewhere. This can only be a winning love combination if the two take the time to really get to know one another. A good love match and a decent marriage are possible, but not probable.

Love Planets: Venus and Mercury

Sun sign combinations are just the tip of the iceberg. You'll want to take a closer look at other factors in your chart to understand the complete you. For example, your Venus is your real love sign—how you see love, what you look for in a mate, and how you deal with sensuality. Mercury, on the other hand, is the planet of communication and intelligence. Good love matches depend on good communication and Mercury compatibility. First, check out the tables in the back of this book and discover if one of your other planets (or your mate's) is in Aries. Then read on.

Venus in Aries

You're not much of a homebody if your Venus is in this sign. On the contrary, you're always out and about—making love and war. You don't like to be controlled in love, and you get annoyed when a partner is nitpicky, pessimistic, or a general party pooper. Venus in Aries rarely makes for a faithful creature. These people love sex to be wild, exciting, and a little dangerous. To win over a person with Venus in Aries, play hard to get. Venus in Aries goes with Venus signs in Leo, Sagittarius, Libra, Aries, and Capricorn.

Mercury in Aries

They're smart, and they expect you to be. Though easily impressed, they'll change their mind about you in a flash—so watch out! Aries in Mercury is instinctively a good communicator and will always know the right way to approach a subject. Though they'll entertain long debates only if they deem you worthy of their time, Aries in Mercury are knowledgeable about many things.

You'll be impressed with the range of interests expressed. Though always out to be right, this person isn't difficult to communicate with. Good combinations with Mercury in Aries are Mercury in Sagittarius, Leo, Pisces, Virgo, and Taurus.

Chapter 2

Taurus

It's very possible a Taurus has charmed his or her way into your life at one time or another. Interesting, playful, sensitive, and romantic, Bulls make great friends, lovers, husbands, wives, and parents. Everyone knows the Bull is also not likely to take "no" for an answer, but what about his other, lesser-known traits? For a deeper understanding of sexy, hard-headed Taurus, read on.

The Conqueror

Put a Bull in a room full of those of the opposite sex, and he's likely to work the entire place without breaking a sweat. He's a huge flirt, so you may not want to leave him alone in a room with your best friend, either— though if he's committed to you, his moves will be all huff and no puff. In other words, a Taurus will take his relationship responsibilities seriously. He's out to conquer, so if he's already won you over, he'll do his best to keep you. Unlike his predecessor in the zodiac, Aries, he's not just out for the game of it. He wants a long-term partner—marriage and the works. And if he hasn't already made you his, he's not likely to stop until he's done so.

I Want It and I'll Get It!

In this respect, Taurus can sometimes seem like a spoiled child who wants what she wants when she wants it. She can get obsessive if there's someone who won't give her the time of day. And once you're hers, she's likely to think of you as a possession—a prize she's won. In other words, she'll be jealous and quite possessive if you're given to flirting, even for fun.

In fact, watch out! Both Taurus men and women scorned are like eyes of a storm—seemingly quiet while creating chaos around them on all sides. You won't want to make a Taurus angry. He'll lash out at you, perhaps even saying nasty things that he will absolutely not take back. Some signs forgive and forget, like Pisces or Cancer. Some signs forgive but don't forget (like Leo,

Sagittarius, or Scorpio). And some signs, like Taurus, will neither forgive nor forget. If you've wronged him once, he won't give you another chance to do it again. He'll take his cards and lay them out on someone else's table.

 ALERT!

> Like Aries (though perhaps more so with Taurus), the Bull wants security above all. If he feels he can't trust you, he won't waste his time investing his feelings in you. With Taurus, always do the right thing from the start.

Secret Traits

So there you have it. Taurus, both men and women, are charmers and great talkers. They have a wide range of interests and are, many times, avid readers. Most Taurus people keep up with politics and international news. Another thing not widely known about Taurus is that she has to fall in love with your mind. While her body may tell her otherwise, it's not enough for you to be attractive and desirable to her. She's also on the lookout for a partner who can keep up with her both mentally and physically.

Actually, Taurus is the most physical sign of the zodiac—in bed. Though Taurus is a natural sportsman, like Aries and Sagittarius, his sensuality in the bedroom is highly attuned. Like Scorpio, who is sexually instinctive but less romantic and more intense, Taurus has a sexual appetite heartier than all other signs. He also needs to dominate, both between the sheets and out. But he's more into the service aspect of making love—your needs will always come before his own.

 ESSENTIAL

> With Taurus, having his ego pumped up and intact is nearly as essential as breathing. He'll want to please you because it makes him feel like "a real man." You'll always feel taken care of with a Bull—male or female.

You Can't Hurry Love

Here's a sign who likes to take her time with things. She'll want you to be totally devoted to her, but she wants freedom to make up her mind about you when she's ready. If a Taurus feels she is being rushed in a relationship, she'll get even more stubborn and absolutely won't budge. For her, love must be a process: the wooing, the getting-to-know, the coming-to-terms, the agreements and disagreements, the commitment, and the final step—marriage. Taurus can sometimes be in a relationship for years before actually getting to the altar.

The Old-Fashioned Type

In fact, Taurus people are the most old-fashioned of the zodiac. They're gallant. A Taurus man will wait for you for a year, if need be, if you're not ready to make love with him. He'll consider it an honor. He's a real gentleman, that big romantic Bull. Unfortunately, this can work the other way, too. Go to bed with him too quickly—or even drink too much alcohol in front of him—and he'll judge you for it. Sometimes you may think that if you sat him down with one of your grandparents, the two could go on for hours about "kids these days."

 ALERT!

> Make sure to listen when your Taurus mate talks about others. He's giving you clues about how he wants you to behave—what you should and shouldn't do, and what he considers proper. In this way, you'll get a good idea what your Bull is about.

The Art of Attraction

It would be easy to assume that because Taurus men and women like a good old-fashioned courtship that you should be polite, easygoing, and affectionate with them. Here's a tip: not so. Though it's wrong to play games in love, perhaps, Taurus actually needs a little cruelty in the beginning to get the ball rolling.

In other words, if you come off easy and sweet, your Taurus will not think you're a prize worth winning— he's a conqueror, remember? Now, we're not talking about being mean or vicious, but it's okay to make the big Bull jump through a few hoops. He'll do it, after all. And when he tires of jumping, he'll come around the other side, plant a big kiss on your lips, and you'll see what it's like to be literally swept off your feet. Just make sure you always listen to the Bull. If he feels he's not being heard, he's sure to get cranky.

The Long Haul

Whether or not you'd actually be good for her is not the point. Taurus has a hard time choosing a partner that's right for her. She tends to set her sights on someone more for the security (or the challenge) than for suitability. In fact, the more you tell a Taurus you're not right for her, the more likely she is to pursue you. As mentioned, Taurus has a tough time with "no." She might seem to shy away for a while, while in truth she's just off formulating another plan to get you.

 ALERT!

If you want to get a Bull, don't play coy— think mother or father figure. Be nurturing and then pull away and reprimand Taurus (in the beginning). He'll quickly become attached and aim to win your affections.

When they don't cut themselves off emotionally, a Taurus makes for a wonderful mate, father, or mother.

Sometimes when the Bull is out for something, he holds tight to the security itself, and that becomes his definition of real love. Instinctively, though, he knows how to draw someone to him and how to get someone's affections. True, this is done by simply pulling away. Taurus goes off to sulk, and his partner, who's used to the constant affection, goes after him. But Taurus always provides the constancy that he himself craves for family. Taurus will attempt to ensure everyone's happiness around him.

He/She: The Little Stuff Counts

Taurus likes expensive, tailored clothing and likes you to be dressed well, too. Like their ideals, they tend to lean toward the conservative side. For a woman, a little sexy is okay, as long as it isn't overdone. Though Taurus man may seem to like it, he'll be silently wondering if you've dressed like this for him or for everyone else in the room. Be safe, and take a sweater along to drape over that sexy black dress. This will impress Taurus.

Master of Perception

Here's another kicker. Taurus is very good at discovering your little secrets—the ones he's interested in. He'll play it cool and subtly get the information out of you. Then he'll file it away and use it as ammunition when he needs it. On the surface, Taurus comes off as calm and noncritical, going along with whatever you say. Deep down, though, he's playing all kinds of scenarios in his head.

For example, if you call a Taurus man and tell him about breaking up with your ex, he may laugh and side with you. But he won't answer the next time you call. It's that simple. Taurus makes no exceptions. Keep in mind that when a Taurus asks questions, the inquiries are always indirectly linked with security—having to do with relationship, money, or something else.

The Money Factor

Here's how to get rid of a Taurus quickly: Tell her you have a little bit of a spending problem. You try to manage your finances well, and you try not to spend even though you're in debt, but you just can't seem to stop. Don't be surprised if Taurus's head spins around and rolls off her shoulders. Actually, chances are that you won't get any reaction. As mentioned before, Taurus is great at hiding distaste. Eventually, it will come out, but not usually in the moment.

 ESSENTIAL

Many famous astrologers characterize Taurus as "materialistic." In truth, money for Taurus is not as much for luxury as it is for security. For Taurus, money is freedom, freedom is security, and security is happiness.

Don't be surprised if the Bull romances you with expensive theater tickets or a candlelight dinner for two at the hottest restaurant in town. Because money is so important to Taurus, he'll think it's important to you, too. Unfortunately, though, Taurus's generosity does not normally stem from an infectious need to give (as it does, let's say, with Leo). Taurus expects something for his efforts. If he's spending a lot of money on you, he's not doing it for the fun of it or because this is the way he would treat himself (like Leo does). He's spending it to win you. If you're not seriously interested in the Bull, leave him alone and look elsewhere. He'll only get surly and nasty if he thinks he's being used.

 ALERT!

> Taurus needs to get emotional with a partner. He goes into things heart and soul. Remember that deep down, he's a romantic. He'll want you to appreciate his efforts for it.

Pillow Talk: Signs in the Bedroom

Getting Taurus into bed is not always easy. Taurus wants to make love—not just have sex. And she'll have to be in love to do that. It's important here to keep in mind that Taurus often falls in love with partners who are not in love with her.

Making love to Taurus is an art. He's not interested solely in the final outcome. Foreplay is genuine and an important prelude to the final act. He'll instinctively know how to warm you up, too. Both Taurus men and Taurus women are true sex kittens—they wrote the book. Following are the differences between seducing a Taurus man and the female Bull.

The Secret Taurus Man

Taurus man does, indeed, take himself a bit too seriously. The weight of the world is on his shoulders, and it's up to him to judge everyone. The whole financial security thing is not a joke—Taurus, no matter how much he's in love, will run away from a partner if he believes she has spending or debt problems. That said, one thing that will help you seduce the male Bull is to spend money on him (at the same time making clear, of course, that doing so does not cause you even the slightest hardship). Take him to an expensive restaurant, or do the opposite. Take him to a less expensive restaurant and show him how good you are at budgeting. He'll appreciate it.

 ALERT!

Though patience is one of Taurus's identifying traits, he'll react with quick, determined impatience if you threaten his sense of constancy— financially or otherwise. When this happens, make amends immediately. And don't do it physically. Repair the problem with words.

The Right Approach

Taurus man will withdraw physically faster than any other sign. If he's hurt, you'll know it right away. He's sensitive. Also remember that Taurus gets a bit obsessive and has a tendency to sink into a depressive state when he's angry or feels he's been betrayed.

Don't try to woo a Taurus back to bed to make it up to him. He'll be offended. Instead, deal with the issue right away, and don't go to sleep mad. If he has time to dwell on things, he'll be worse off the next day and the day after that. Once you've done your job, though, and Taurus forgives you (a difficult task!) you'll be surprised by how fast he'll warm right back up.

 FACT

Physically, Taurus men are usually broad-shouldered and can sometimes be stocky. They love to eat and to watch a woman eat, too. A little extra meat on a woman is not a turnoff for the male Bull.

Making Love

In bed, these men love to bite and be bitten. They love all earthy, sensual qualities of lovemaking. Rub his neck to get him in the mood—it won't take long. Here's a tip: Though the Taurus man needs to dominate in bed, he feels strong and confident enough in his abilities to take direct orders. In fact, when a male Bull is told what to do in bed, it turns him on. Remember that he is service oriented. He'll want you to "finish," like every other project he takes on in life. And Taurus man will do everything he can to get you there. He also always likes to be appreciated for his efforts—he'll want equal attention to all parts of him. Just keep in mind that if you don't finish every time, Taurus will be offended and go away upset.

The Secret Taurus Woman

She's strong and sensual and very stubborn. If you push too hard or too fast, she'll balk. Vulgarity is a huge turnoff for her. Though she seems to be even more aggressive and modern in her approach to sex than her male counterpart, she's just as old-fashioned. In other words, she'll tempt you and tease you into bed, but she's secretly hoping you'll be man enough to stop and tell her you want to wait for the right moment. This will prove that you really care for her.

 ESSENTIAL

With the Taurus woman, everything is a test. Don't take her to bed too quickly. Though it may seem that's what she wants—she may even follow through—she'll only judge you for it. Patience is the key to her heart.

Stability Seeker

Though Taurus man sometimes spins in circles trying to make enough money to appease his insatiable hunger for security, Taurus woman intuitively knows how to earn it and keep it. She'll also look for a very stable provider—wealth can be an aphrodisiac for her. True, she'll fall in love with a man who's not *rich* rich, but she'll never settle down with a man who can't take care of her and her future brood. She looks forward to being a parent; she has an earthy, nurturing instinct that comes out. If she wants to, let her mother you a little.

 QUESTION?

> **What is a great date for a Taurus woman?**
> Anything that makes her feel pampered. Take her out to a beautiful restaurant to wine and dine her. If she lets you into her house (a sure sign that she likes you; Taurus is territorial), cook for her. She may even fall in love with you for it.

Emotional/Physical Connection

Like the male Bull, the female Bull, unfortunately, gets attached to circumstances and misses out on emotions. In other words, her feelings are directly linked to the relationship in terms of what it can give her (security) instead of what she really needs (genuine love and getting to fully know the man behind it all).

She, too, can get a bit obsessed with unrequited love and can quickly fall into a depressive state. Sometimes bed may be the only way to reach her when she becomes emotionally distant and talking doesn't help.

The Proper Treatment

Taurus woman also likes to bite and be bitten. She tends to shy away from very lean, skinny men. She wants to feel protected, and a big, hulking man is what she's likely to look for. Also, she might go for men who are well endowed. This is sometimes important to her. A Taurus woman can go for a little wildness in bed, but she also likes it sweet and slow. Focus on her neck, her buttocks, the back of her legs, and her chest; stay away from her stomach.

Sun Love Matches

Taurus, both man and woman, looks for a mate who will help keep an outwardly calm, tranquil appearance. Inside, they're often roiling with self-doubt and confusion. They shy away from partners who contest their way of handling things and try to dominate them (Fire signs), as well as who give too much ambiguity, and who like to pick a fight with them for fun (Air signs). Following are the love sign combinations with the female Bull.

Taurus Man

Physically, sexually, morally, and idealistically, these two make a great match. They share the same sense of commitment and family responsibility, and both want the security that they can give each other. This can be a great long-term relationship, with marriage probable.

 ESSENTIAL

> Both male and female Bulls are unnaturally stubborn with a fondness for playing leader. Taurus woman can sometimes be insensitive to Taurus man's needs, but Taurus woman is just and Taurus man will appreciate that.

Gemini Man

With Gemini man, Taurus woman won't know whether she's coming or going. This will drive her crazy. In fact, she may just develop an unhealthy attachment to the sense of excitement Gemini gives her. She also expects him to be more ambitious and career oriented. For Gemini, this is too much pressure. Intellectually, the two are well matched. In bed, both are sensual, but Gemini is more fascinated with the fantasy than with the reality of it. They might have a good affair, even a possible long-term relationship, but marriage isn't likely.

Cancer Man

Cancer man can start off shy. If Taurus woman doesn't come on too strong, he'll eventually open up to her. Both want a beautiful home, to spend lots of quiet time there. Sexually, these two are a good match if the female Bull doesn't order the Crab around too much. Both crave trust and are possessive and jealous. If their mood swings don't clash too much, and Taurus woman can stay sensitive to Cancer's needs, the two can have a decent long-term relationship. They can also possibly have a good marriage, albeit one with plenty of drama.

Leo Man

Taurus woman is completely taken in by Leo man's exuberance and good looks. Unfortunately, though Leo man knows how to make money, he also knows how to spend it. This worries Taurus woman, who'd prefer to build a nest egg than go out to dinner every night. Sexually, these two are an incredible match. Taurus woman excites Leo man and the female Bull loves that he is adventurous, intense, and playful in bed. This is a possible long-term relationship but not a probable marriage.

 QUESTION?

What would a Taurus/Leo celebrity couple look like?
Michelle Pfeiffer (Taurus) and Al Pacino (Leo), from the movie *Frankie and Johnny*, is one pair. Other stars who would make interesting mates include Robert De Niro (Leo), Barbara Streisand (Taurus), Dustin Hoffman (Leo), Audrey Hepburn (Taurus), and Arnold Schwarzenegger (Leo).

Virgo Man

Taurus and Virgo go together. Spiritually, they make each other laugh and can have lots of fun together. They're also both insightful and determined—accomplishing whatever task they put their minds to. If Virgo man will stop being righteous with Taurus woman, lovemaking for these two can be erotic, wild, and intense. Taurus is also wowed by Virgo's strange ideas and know-how when it comes to business and making money. She trusts him. This can be an excellent long-term partnership, with marriage a good possibility.

Libra Man

If there's one thing Libra man loves, it's beauty. And Taurus woman is always beautiful in some way. They rarely fight because they both detest confrontation.

 FACT

In terms of commitment, Libra man and Taurus woman flounder around on all fronts: relationship, jobs, and so on. If they can come to more resolute decisions, they make a great team.

If confrontations do happen, they're frequently solved in bed. Sexually, these two can move mountains, though Taurus likes to have sex more often than Libra man. Taurus and Libra makes for a probable long-term relationship with a good chance for marriage.

Scorpio Man

The two together are so intense, passionate, and deep that people around them sometimes feel they've just entered a minefield—or a Greek tragedy. Both have a tendency to feel a bit sorry for themselves, and they're both moody. If they can strike a good balance and not be so dramatic, they can be good together. In bed, their sensuality and sense of adventure reach new heights—though Scorpio, secretly, would prefer to lead a bit more. These two can have a probable long-term relationship and a probable marriage as well.

Sagittarius Man

Sagittarius man is pensive, and Taurus woman likes this. She admires his ability to do anything he wants and wishes she could be more open to the adventures he experiences firsthand.

 ESSENTIAL

> Unfortunately, many Sagittarius men are too modest about their abilities and don't ask for enough compensation for their work. This bothers Taurus. She is also easily hurt by his quick, honest tongue.

Though Sagittarius will take the back seat sometimes to Taurus's desire to lead, he still believes he knows best and can be sarcastic about it, too. In bed, these two are good as long as Sagittarius can let himself feel the emotions that go along with the lovemaking. This is a possible long-term partnership, not a probable marriage.

Capricorn Man

Capricorn is likely to fall in love with Taurus woman. It seems she's the one he's always searched for. Unfortunately, they do have their differences. Though the two hate conflict of any kind, they can get into fights over issues of trust or money. Also, Capricorn man likes to feel he's in control. Taurus woman shakes his stable ground. In bed, Capricorn man can be more interested in what the act signifies itself than in his own sensuality. If these two can find a good balance, though, this is a probable long-term partnership, with marriage a possibility.

Aquarius Man

This is a real case of "opposites attract." You won't find a stranger couple—they're odd together, and it seems to work. Aquarius man brings out the wildness in Taurus woman, and she loves this about him. Though both are incredible flirts, Taurus woman worries a bit that Aquarius man will stray—and he might. But if there's one who can keep him faithful, it's the female Bull. Also, Taurus woman gets mad at Aquarius man's calm, cool, "go-with-the-flow" attitude. These two also have a superficiality hurdle to get over, which requires them to put their priorities into place. Sexually, they're both adventurous and can have fun in bed. This is a probable relationship and a very possible marriage.

 ESSENTIAL

Aquarius men like strangeness in the bedroom. If Taurus woman can let go of her old-fashioned side a bit, Aquarius man will be more taken by her. Aquarius needs to be wild and, many times, wouldn't mind experimenting with sex toys.

Pisces Man

Taurus woman is drawn to Pisces' sense of tranquility, his emotional depth, and his instinctive ways. She should trust him more on his judgment of people. Taurus, though, is able to relax and be herself with Pisces man even if she can't always take the criticism Pisces doles out. Fortunately, Pisces knows how to word his views just the right way. In bed, Pisces man lets Taurus woman take the lead, and the two play well together. If they can just stop manipulating each other at times, this pair makes for a possible long-term relationship, though not a likely marriage.

Aries Man

Aries man sweeps Taurus woman off her feet. The two are social, but Aries man needs more diversity than

Taurus woman, who wants simple constancy. The issue of trust comes up between these two a lot. Aries is not half as possessive or emotionally reckless as Taurus woman. Also, Taurus woman is so wowed by Aries man, she doesn't stop to think if she's in love with him or just in love with the idea of him. In bed, things are great. Chances are that this is a probable long-term relationship but not a good idea for marriage.

 FACT

> When you think of Taurus women, think of strong women who can really take care of themselves. Here are some famous female Bulls: Audrey Hepburn, Ella Fitzgerald, Katherine Hepburn, Queen Mary II, and Eva Peron (Evita).

Love Planets: Venus and Mercury

If Venus or Mercury is in Taurus for you or for your mate, make sure to read the entire Taurus chapter. Every nuance of Taurus is included and will help you understand the sign and its influences more comprehensively. Venus and Mercury dates are at the back of the book. Read the charts, and match yours accordingly. Taurus in any person's chart will always add an obstinate nature, a need for security, and an interest in finance. For more precise information, read on.

Venus in Taurus

Though you may like to travel, coming home to a stable, tranquil environment is what you always look forward to. Family is very important, and you strive to be a good parent. You search for a love partner who will give you security and who will be faithful—it would be wonderful if he or she were a great cook, too! Infidelity is something you absolutely won't tolerate. When other people tell you about your choice of love mate, listen. They sometimes know better about what's best for you. Venus in Taurus goes well with Venus in Virgo, Taurus, Capricorn, Cancer, and Scorpio.

Mercury in Taurus

Intellectually, you know how to express yourself. You may be drawn to jobs of a more technical nature. If not, your artistic edge could come out on the stage or in writing. People are impressed with the way you handle yourself professionally, but you have a tough time with authority and don't necessarily stay long in any office job. Working freelance suits your tastes. You're interested more in the way things work than why they do. You're realistic, practical, and (though a touch romantic) despise a mate who seems to live in a fantasy world. You wouldn't mind letting someone change your mind for you, but nobody can ever quite do it. Mercury in Taurus goes well with Mercury in Virgo, Taurus, Capricorn, Libra, Gemini, and Sagittarius.

Chapter 3
Gemini

Gemini is so crafty, so devilish . . . so delightful—and you think you've really gotten to know him? You could be mistaken. Gemini is the most unpredictable of all the signs in the zodiac. In fact, the only thing you can count on with the Twin is that you can't really count on anything. In this chapter, learn the tricks of the Twin and Gemini's deepest, darkest secrets.

The Born Storyteller

No one can tell a story like Gemini. She'll have everyone in the room hanging on her every word. Of course, every tale is a little bit better when it's changed, exaggerated, and embellished. Actually, it may just be complete blarney. But that's okay. That's what's expected from Gemini. It's part of her charm.

Gemini can easily charm people of the opposite sex, true. But he'll also flirt with anyone who happens to be in front of him—friends, children, or the elderly. He does it for fun and because it's second nature to him. In fact, Gemini will always have a horde of fans at any given time.

 FACT

Gemini needs to be adored and considers it her birthright. She knows she's sexy and that others dig her—and she's always prepared to use her assets to help her out in any situation.

Moody Outbursts

Gemini gets bored easily. She changes her mind constantly and expects you to keep up. She can be unrealistic, and she frequently unwittingly sabotages close, personal relationships. She also gets distracted when the conversation doesn't revolve around something she's interested in.

Gemini, you should know, can display a bit of a violent nature if she feels betrayed. Chances are, she's only out for the drama of it—but do yourself a favor and expect to have the phone hung up on you if she's angry. Plus, she may play a little verbal hardball with you before she's done. Don't worry, though. Gemini also forgives and forgets faster than any other sign.

 ALERT!

> Don't try to make up with hotheaded Gemini when he's angry—he'll cut you down to size. Give him some breathing room and time to think. He'll come back to you with an apology— if he's wrong—before the day is over.

Twin's Generous Side

Shortcomings aside, Gemini is one of the more generous of signs. She gives great advice and knows exactly what to say to cheer you up—even if her comfort is a bit unorthodox. Really, Gemini is a great friend and also gives every bit of her soul to a love relationship. Actually, she sometimes gives too much of herself. She's confident and will lay her cards on the table, perhaps a little too soon. But that doesn't seem to bother anyone who's falling for a Gemini. Instead, most members of the opposite sex feel lucky to have her. She's a wild card—funny, exciting, and beautiful—and yet sometimes off her rocker (in a good way). True, she can even be flaky at times. But one thing is for sure: No one is ever bored with the erratic Twin.

Split Personality

So how is it possible to predict what a Gemini will do next when he, himself, doesn't know? It's not easy. One moment he seems to like you, while the next moment he's ignoring you—chatting away with his buddy. What should you do? Well, for starters, remember that in terms of needing a good challenge, Gemini is as bad as Aries. Aries, though, is more interested in the chase, whereas Gemini is curious about the possibilities. Gemini loves to always leave a few options open. The excitement of "Will I or won't I?" always plays a part in the Twin drama of the moment.

 QUESTION?

How do you get Gemini's attention?
In the beginning, don't flirt too much. Flirting indicates you're interested. In Gemini's mind, she's already conquered you. Show her you can have a good conversation and talk to others. If she wants you, she'll find you and make her play.

The Love Game

The saying "split personality" really applies to Gemini on all levels. He's not easy to figure out right away, and you'll hurt your head trying. Just when you feel like the two of you have clicked, he'll pull away. He can even seem a little obsessive at times, but he's nothing like Taurus, Cancer, or Scorpio. For him, it's all part of the love game. Here are a few examples:

- Gemini romances you all night, and then leaves without saying goodbye.
- Gemini is always there for you, but the one time you need him the most, he's off resolving another "situation."
- Gemini seems very sensitive and then suddenly appears frighteningly cold and apathetic.
- He lets you cry for hours on his shoulder and then blames you for being a wuss.
- Gemini picks a best buddy to hang around with, and then tells you about his friend's shortcomings.
- Gemini dates the least appropriate person within a mile's radius—especially when people tell him not to.
- He calls you a million times in one day and then tells you you're being insecure if you ever do the same.

As you can see, it's not easy keeping a Gemini blissful. But as a lover, Gemini knows no bounds. He's extremely affectionate to his one and only—when he gets around to choosing her.

 FACT

Gemini needs to be out and about. She needs to be social. If she's all work and no play, she's just not a happy camper.

Gemini can't go for a long time without being in love. He doesn't like to stay alone. You will almost never find two- or three-month stretches when the most exciting entry in his calendar reads "Get up, feed dog, go to work, come home, eat dinner, go to sleep."

The Twin's View on Work

Most Geminis, in fact, don't really like to work. They do it for their sense of dignity or for money and prestige, but it's rarely because they actually enjoy it. For Gemini, work is a means to an end. Many Gemini women wouldn't mind taking off from work and having their husbands take care of them. Of course, they'd be bored in no time. And, heaven forbid that their husbands might ask them to pick up a vacuum and clean—that would be the end of their time in the house.

The Art of Attraction

Gemini practically oozes sex. Man or woman, Gemini has sex appeal that could conquer entire countries. In fact, if you want to make a good impression in any situation, bring a Gemini along. He'll know exactly what to say and how to say it.

 ESSENTIAL

Gemini can get along with anybody (if she's so inclined). If not, a verbal lash or a little sarcasm might just be how a Gemini flirts. Read on to learn what makes a Gemini tick and how to get her hooked.

The Long Haul

Most Geminis get married later in life. They claim that they'd like to settle down and raise a family—yet they either find this or that wrong with their potential mates. Better still, they have long-term relationships with people they know are simply not suitable for the long haul. Chances are, though, they're more worried about what tomorrow will bring than what lies fifteen years in the future.

Gemini tends to fall in love with the person who makes him laugh. He's extremely witty and wants his partner to be, too. Remember that he's an Air sign, so he's got to be conquered first through his mind. He always goes for someone "cool"—daring and exciting.

 ALERT!

> A homebody will not impress Gemini. She'll want to be out on the town, and she'll want you to take her there. This will probably not change over time.

He/She: The Little Stuff Counts

Gemini women like to dress on the sexy side. At the very least, they'll wear something to go along with their fun, flirty personalities. Gemini men, on the other hand, are stylish and sexy no matter what they wear. They're not particularly conservative. They go along with the latest style, as long as it's not too trendy or weird. The Gemini man doesn't mind a bit of sexiness in his partner—as long as it's tasteful.

 ESSENTIAL

> Gemini men and women take great care in their appearance. A compliment will go a long way. In fact, you'll get extra points if you notice a new shirt, suit, or dress.

Showing Off

Gemini men and women both like to show off the partner on their arm. If a Gemini introduces you to all his friends, you should know he really likes you. His friends are his lifeline. But love is always important to a Gemini. He falls in love quickly, it's true, but whether it's *true* love, only time will tell. If it's not, a Gemini will be out the door faster than you can say "fickle."

The Big Spender

When it comes to money, Gemini tends to spend more money on his partner than on himself. He's usually generous and doesn't expect anything for it (except your constant devotion and loyalty!). As far as wanting something for his efforts, this is understandable. Gemini needs a partner who keeps him guessing but one he also knows he can count on. Anyway, it's not easy getting away with treating a Gemini badly. He knows exactly how to work you and get back your affections.

Playing Games

When it comes to playing games, Gemini invented the rules. A less evolved Gemini will be a little needy, possessive, and manipulative. But in the end, she'll still get what she wants. Beware, though, of a clingy Gemini. This tends to be the type who can get violent if provoked. A more evolved Gemini, on the other hand, will come close to giving the appearance of an Earth sign. She'll be interesting, fair, and emotionally balanced—a wonderful lover and partner.

 FACT

Gemini is also open to mates of very different background, race, religion, and even age. It's not uncommon for a Gemini to date a person much older or much younger than he is.

Pillow Talk: Signs in the Bedroom

Gemini is definitely able to separate sex, love, flings, and real relationships. If she gets it in her mind that you're nothing more than a roll in the hay, she's not likely to change her mind and let it develop into something more meaningful. Gemini is also very sexual but not very sensual (like Scorpio and Taurus). This means that slow, languorous sex is probably not on the menu for the evening.

Actually, Gemini goes for the strange and interesting in the bedroom. Nothing is out of bounds or considered taboo. Gemini also likes to be seduced. A conservative "let's have sex" line will absolutely not work on a Gemini. The Twin goes for a flirty, sexy smile and deep, dark eye contact. Gemini is an expert in the seduction category and expects you to be the same.

 ALERT!

> Don't necessarily run away from a Gemini who's just insulted you! This is what he wants—he's testing you. Gemini men were the ones who pulled your ponytails in class. Strangely enough, it may be the one way he shows he likes you.

The Secret Gemini Man

Gemini man, on the whole, doesn't know what he wants. If you look at a list of his past relationships, you may have a problem finding a particular pattern to his conquests. Instead, his ex-girlfriends only have one thing in common: They're all completely different. But one thing is true—he's most likely the one who walked away from the relationship first.

Seducing the Twin

As said before, Gemini really gets turned on with the mind. Serve up some good wine, make some good conversation, and demonstrate you understand who the people around you are. That will impress a Gemini man and make him like you more. There's not much you can do to seduce a Gemini man into bed, though. He has decided before the evening even started whether he plans to take you to bed. Though Gemini is sexual, he can also be extremely logical.

Pleasure in Bed

Once in the bedroom, though, Gemini man is adventurous and crafty. He's a fantastic kisser and he likes doing it. He'll need to vary positions to keep his interest up. And Gemini can be a bit sexually selfish, too. This time without words, you can guide Gemini to make him understand what you want. Gemini will pick up your cue easily. A lot of eye contact in bed helps a Gemini man focus on you and on the matter at hand.

The Secret Gemini Woman

She can be wild in bed. Once she's given herself over to you, she'll expect all kinds of sexy moves and seduction. You'll feel like Gemini is grading you—and she is. Conservative positions don't necessarily tickle her fancy. She's looking for style, flair, and imagination.

 FACT

For Gemini woman, great lovemaking is important. She'll leave a relationship that doesn't have it and stay way too long in a relationship that does.

Sex Talk

Sometimes she likes dirty talk in bed—other times, she might want you to say nothing at all. Ask her what mood she's in. She'll tell you. Most Gemini women carry their verbal skills into the bedroom in some way, even if it's just to give an occasional "ooh" or "aah" to let you know you're doing just fine.

Gemini woman is more easily seduced than Gemini man. Though she's probably decided before the night has started whether she'll allow herself to trip the lights fantastic with you, she can be swayed with sexy conversation (including what you'd like to do with her if you got your way). She'll also be impressed with a little flash—a sleek car, trendy ethnic restaurant, important friends, and some casual name-dropping will help further your cause.

 ALERT!

Gemini women tend to be on the jealous side. Watch out! If she sees you talking to your ex at a party, not only will you miss out on getting lucky—you just might have a first-rate drama on your hands.

Playing It Safe

Okay, so Gemini women like to create scenes. Their tendency to exhibitionism has a mind of its own. Did you ever see a man get a drink thrown in his face or a woman screaming at him at the top of her lungs in public? Chances are it was a Gemini woman creating the chaos. It's best not to provoke a Gemini woman. Play it safe and keep her happy, and your time with her will remain copacetic.

Sun Love Matches

Gemini tends to fall for rogues, Casanova types, man-eaters, or lady-killers. Gemini woman will always look for a "difficult" partner—one who has a sharp tongue and who is not easy to control. She basically has two types: anyone she can lead around and tell what to do, and anyone who will dominate her. The latter has a better chance of winning her heart. Read on to learn about the love-sign matches for the female Twin.

Gemini Man

These two like to gossip, play, and get into trouble together. They sometimes get into cat-and-dog fights only to turn around, kiss, and make up. Don't bother siding with one of them because they're more likely to forgive each other and consider you a traitor. In fact, they're each other's sounding board. Their connection is deep because it's based on the mind (and good sex). Unfortunately, neither is extremely adept at earning money and keeping it. They have great ideas, but they are likely to start a project and never finish it. However, these two make a probable long-term relationship and have a good chance for marriage.

FACT

> Gemini signs will be instantly attracted to each
> other—even if it's only for a secret, steamy
> affair. A good example of this could be Marilyn
> Monroe and President John F. Kennedy (both
> Geminis).

Cancer Man

These two can be manipulative and sneaky with a
tendency to play dirty—and they actually like this about
one another. Things are definitely not boring between
them. Unfortunately, Cancer doesn't always trust Gemini
woman on many levels. She flirts with others too much
for his taste. She tells little fibs here and there and
seems a bit detached from her feelings at times. Cancer
man could teach her many things, but Gemini woman
won't let him. Both can be possessive and moody
although Gemini can be quickly snapped out of a bad
mood while Cancer can't. This bothers Gemini woman.
She also likes to go out on the town more than the
Crab. In bed, both are adventurous, but Cancer wants
Gemini to prove her feelings run deeper than he suspects. This can be a long-term relationship but not a
probable marriage.

Leo Man

Leo man finds Gemini to be refreshing, exciting,
interesting, and witty. No one can make Leo laugh like

Gemini. Though he finds her antics amusing, he slowly tires of them. The two challenge each other, but Leo doesn't like liars, however harmless. Both know how to play the game and keep each other guessing. Leo gives Gemini the kind of loyalty she needs, but Gemini has a hard time doing the same for Leo man. She loves the fact that he's generous with money. In bed, things can be utter paradise or complete hell—depending on whether the two stay on the same level during the relationship. If they can find a good balance, this might be a possible long-term partnership or marriage.

 ESSENTIAL

> Gemini woman runs if she feels pressured or suffocated in a relationship. Leo man instinctively knows how to treat her with kid gloves. If he provokes her, chances are he's looking for an easy way to escape the relationship himself.

Virgo Man

It's difficult to be around these two when they bicker. Verbally, they can be cutting and harsh. In fact, if there's any man who can reduce Gemini woman to tears, it's Virgo man. She'll have to develop a thicker skin to be with him. Intellectually, though, these two can talk 'til morning. They know how to amuse one another, and Gemini likes Virgo's attentive, instinctive style in bed. Also, if Gemini can convince Virgo to give way to his natural sexual tendencies, these two can go for hours and hours without coming up for air (that is, if they ever make it to the bed). Unfortunately though, Virgo can sometimes bring out the worst in Gemini woman. She'll purposely provoke and irritate him for the fun of it, and the relationship will end. This is a possible long-term relationship but not a recommended marriage.

Libra Man

Together, these two are wickedly mischievous. Gemini woman is impressed with Libra's sense of style and flair. She loves his eyes and his long, sexy stares. She'll be curious to figure him out. Both like to be worshipped in bed and, though the sex can be masterful, Libra man sometimes wishes Gemini woman would be a little more soft and shy for him. This would make him more comfortable. This is a probable long-term relationship, and there's an excellent chance for marriage if Libra man can "tame" Gemini woman to his liking.

 FACT

Libra is not as cool and calm as he seems to be. His silent treatments make her nervous and may make her a bit aggressive. Libra also likes to avoid conflict, while Gemini searches it out.

Scorpio Man

When Scorpio falls, he falls hard. In the beginning, he'll give Gemini woman the attention she needs. He'll call when he's supposed to and treat her like a queen. But this affection may dwindle after awhile or even stop completely. Gemini woman also doesn't have the means or the inclination to figure out Scorpio's hidden agenda. The two can go in circles with verbal games. Also, Gemini can't stand Scorpio's bad moods. Scorpio, though, has just the right blend of passion and moves in bed for finicky Gemini. If she goes to bed with him, she'll keep coming back for more. They have a somewhat decent chance for a long-term relationship, but they're not likely to marry.

Sagittarius Man

Gemini woman and Sagittarius man sometimes make a great couple because when Sagittarius becomes quiet, Gemini keeps the conversation going. True, Gemini is a bit too flighty for Sagittarius's tastes, and he also doesn't always trust her. Together, though, they can travel around the world and have amazing experiences. Unfortunately, Gemini woman doesn't always take his advice, and this bothers him. She can also get possessive, which he also definitely doesn't like. In bed, though, these two create fireworks. If Gemini can remain emotionally stable, it's probable these two will have a long-term thing and, beyond that, marriage is possible.

Capricorn Man

Capricorn man doesn't believe a single thing that comes out of Gemini's mouth—and he shouldn't. She purposely shocks him and provokes him for kicks. He's too easy a target for her. This combination really depends upon what is in the rest of Capricorn's chart. If he is especially earthy, forget it. If he has a lot of Air and Fire, this can be a good match. Gemini inspires Capricorn to make money and try new things. Capricorn, on the other hand, grounds Gemini. If she takes him seriously, these two can conquer worlds together. In bed, Gemini tends to be a bit wilder than the Goat, and she may grow tired of his more conservative approach to lovemaking. This can be a possible long-term partnership, but it's not a probable marriage.

 ALERT!

The easiest downfall for Capricorn with Gemini is that the Twin likes to talk about the relationship (and maybe even the sex). Capricorn will avoid these conversations at all costs! This makes Gemini nervous. Eventually, this problem will fester and become bigger than the love partnership itself.

Aquarius Man

These two make a great team. Finally, Aquarius man has found a woman who excites him and can keep him on his toes. Though Aquarius is a bit more grounded than Gemini woman, the two together can still get into plenty of mischief. Fun is a key word here. Laughter is another. They both have the same style in and out of bed. Aquarius man, though, can sometimes be a bit too strange for Gemini (but she may just appreciate this, too). If these two stay away from superficial matters and get their priorities in order, this can be an excellent long-term relationship and a good marriage after that.

Pisces Man

These two make a strange pair, but it seems to work. Pisces is very quiet, Gemini does all the talking, and neither minds a bit. Pisces provides an outlet through which Gemini can experience the range of her emotions. Pisces has a lot to teach her, and Gemini is curious to learn from mysterious Pisces. If he stays strong and doesn't let Gemini play with his affections, they can be good together. Pisces, though, is a bit more romantic in bed while Gemini is more spontaneous. This can be an interesting couple, though—both in and out of the bedroom. If Gemini doesn't get too clingy and Pisces too withdrawn, they have a possible long-term relationship in store, and then a good chance for marriage.

Aries Man

Aries man knows just how to get Gemini woman interested. One look and she's hooked. Neither one likes to feel pressured or suffocated in a relationship.

But they like going out, being social, and flirting. There's only one problem: Gemini does it for fun, while Aries means it. If Gemini gets possessive, Aries will run the other way. In bed, though, these two are a sexual miracle—fabulous lovers. If Gemini respects Aries preferences for life and the way it should be lived, this is a probable long-term relationship, with a good outlook for marriage.

 ESSENTIAL

> Gemini's little outbursts might bother Aries, and he won't forgive her if she says something nasty to him. However, she won't take it back.

Taurus Man

No matter how hard he tries to figure out Gemini woman, he simply can't get what makes her tick. This will drive him nuts. Just when he imagines things are going smoothly, she shows up late, once again, with a ridiculously flimsy excuse. He lets her get away with it because he can't stand fighting in public. He prays she won't make a scene. Sometimes he's embarrassed by her flamboyant sexual behavior—though he's secretly turned on by it. If Gemini lets him, Taurus can show her a thing or two in bed. Once she's gone to bed with him, Gemini won't easily let Taurus get away. Though this is a strange couple, they can have a possible long-term relationship, though marriage isn't necessarily a good idea.

Love Planets: Venus and Mercury

A Venus or Mercury in Gemini will give you a more inquisitive nature. It also gives an individual better verbal skills and a need to communicate and be heard. Though Gemini is a good talker, he can be a good listener as well. Gemini is more of a friendship sign sometimes than it is a deep love sign. Read on to find out how Gemini affects the stars and planets in your chart.

 ESSENTIAL

> Gemini's standards are high, requiring that any potential partners match his specifications almost point for point. Also, he won't give his partner any hints as to what he's looking for—he expects her to figure it out for herself.

Venus in Gemini

Though many astrologers say that Venus in Gemini can be unfeeling and rationalizes too much, this is simply not so. Gemini in Venus falls in love with love. She has plenty of emotions but doesn't know how to express them. Instead, she has protective barriers up because she's been burned once or twice and refuses to let herself be burned again. In love, Venus in Gemini can change her mind a number of times, but once she's picked a target, she attaches herself to it . . . him! He becomes a fixation. Instead of moping about, pining after him, though, she takes the aggressive route and goes after him. Once she has what she wants, she may not be sure she wants it. If she does, however, she'll dedicate her time solely to him. Venus in Gemini matches with Venus in Aries, Scorpio, Sagittarius, Pisces, Virgo, and Libra.

Mercury in Gemini

Though you're a great talker, your ideas are extreme and go from one end of the spectrum to the other. In fact, you love to be persuaded and may even fall in love with someone who can easily accomplish this almost impossible task. You have good timing and can tell a joke quite well once you get up the nerve to do it. In terms of work, you'd do well writing speeches or scripts for television or the movies. You may even be drawn to a partner who doesn't say a lot because you're convinced there's more to him than meets the eye. You're also not averse to telling a little white lie, when "necessary." It's part of your diplomatic nature. However, you like to be persuaded that your potential mate deserves your faith and trust before you actually give it. Mercury in Gemini can pair well with Mercury in Virgo, Aquarius, Pisces, Aries, Gemini, Leo, Capricorn, and Taurus.

Chapter 4
Cancer

Cancer can almost seem like any other sign of the zodiac. Lucky him! He's got the dominance of a Fire sign, the sensitivity of a Water sign, the sensibility and practicality of an Earth sign, and even the ability to communicate like an Air sign. In this chapter, find out more about adaptable, energetic cardinal Cancer. He's not always the moody, sentimental fool he's made out to be.

The Expansive Heart

Cancer has so much to give. Truly, she's got a heart of gold. She's also surprisingly outgoing and independent—and she's able to show the world what she's made of. In fact, she's definitely not the wallflower some astrologers make her out to be! She's a cardinal sign—meaning, of course, that she secretly likes to dominate. In other words, you won't find a Cancer bowing to another sign. She's regal. She knows how to turn things around to her advantage. Cancer has the world at her fingertips. How she chooses to use this awesome power depends on her.

Cancer's World

Cancers also have incredible insight into dealing with the world. They know when to lay back and when to charge forward. Yes, they can be sly and manipulative. These traits, though, will disappear as they get older and learn. Eventually, they'll be able to somehow fit into society and adhere to its "strict" (to them) social demands.

At the same time, Cancers don't really like to march to the beat of the same drum as others. Though they're not as radical as Aquarians, they do like to go against the grain. Strangely enough, however, Cancers like a partner who fits into a traditional role. While Aquarians search out a mate who definitely can't be pegged into any one category, Cancer wants someone who will meet with the appreciation and approval of his family. Real respect from a Cancer is very hard to come by. It may seem as if he's made you his world, but unless he also wants to make you part of his family, you've got nothing coming. A Cancer will immediately settle down when he finds the one for him.

 ALERT!

> If a Cancer man or woman is stalling to get married, it probably means that it won't happen. Cancer, when he finds the one for him, will not hesitate to procure a ring and rush to the altar. He needs to know his future is set and happily secure.

Maintaining Balance

Here's the key to a happy Cancer life: a regime that lets her be social when she feels like it or to stay at home and hide when she wants. Don't be fooled by gregarious Cancer. She likes her digs as much or more than she likes the bar and "out" life. In fact, tranquility is essential to the Crab. She'll do everything she can in order to maintain this relaxed and idealistic life vision.

Cordial Cancer

Also, Cancers are almost always cordial. They know how to deal with different types of people and how to make them feel comfortable and included. Compliments run freely from the mouths of Cancers. When they choose, they can be effectively politically correct. When they're out and about, they can come off as Fire signs because they're very good at striking up a conversation. They're also quite sexy and charismatic, and they have an exceptional flair for putting outfits together to show off their best assets.

Cancers are also great empathizers. They'll rarely pity someone for bad fortune—Cancer believes you should take charge of the situation and deal with it. They also have two strong, genuine shoulders to cry on. One thing you may notice about Cancer is that she'll tell you what she thinks, but she'll rarely lecture you about anything. Instead, she'll simply say the way things are, according to her. If you've done something wrong, Cancer will be the first to tell you—but only if you ask for advice.

 ESSENTIAL

A Cancer will not give unsolicited information. If, however, you get specific instructions or advice, you should pay attention. Cancer is able to look at the big picture and get a clear understanding of what's going on—things you wouldn't normally notice.

A Fine Romance

Somehow, you always get the feeling that Cancer is giving you compliments simply for the sake of it. You feel special for the moment until, suddenly, the flattery is being handed to the person next to you. How does he manage to always get away with it? Sometimes Cancer doesn't realize that people can see through the image he's created for himself—though this is of no concern. Cancer never suffers for it. Not many are likely to challenge the Crab. Most people, with egos pumped up by Cancer, know that what they're told is not necessarily the truth—but they never seem to mind.

Family and Friends

It is also said that family life and home is very important to Cancers. This is indubitably true. All Cancers are, in some way, tied to family—whether it's their own (husband, wife, children) or immediate (parents, siblings). Marriage and children are essential to most Cancers, and security becomes just as important to Cancer as it is to Capricorn, Taurus, Virgo, and Scorpio.

 FACT

> Cancer adores having dinners at home with other twosomes. If the said couple is having problems, though, Cancer will be the first to shy away. Cancer only likes the company of those who reflect the idealistic vision of what she wants in her own life.

All Cancers are nurturing, especially Cancer woman, who is sexy and always has some kind of feminine quality. This especially comes out with the friends around her. She's like a mother hen, curious about gossip and new loves. In fact, she'll be a little offended if her friends don't keep her up to date on their possible new love interests. Cancer woman absolutely has to know what's going on and what she can do to help keep the ball rolling. In other words, Cancer woman loves having other "in love" couples to hang out with.

The Art of Attraction

Most Cancers tend to see the world through rose-colored glasses. Although they can see many things of life clearly, love doesn't happen to be one of them. This doesn't stop Cancer, however. Unlike many people, he usually finds what he's looking for in a partner. Being wildly swept away is extremely important to Cancer. He wants the romance of a lifetime and usually gets it.

Once Cancer is in love, too, she tends to stay in love. She's good at keeping her mate—she knows just how to give him what he needs. Once she sees what she wants, she grabs on and doesn't give up so easily. She feels, therefore she is. However, if she's jilted, it may also take her a long time to let go.

The Long Haul

Needless to say, Cancer makes a wonderful love partner and parent. He dotes, and he's affectionate. He might even cook up a storm. He has lots of interesting friends from all walks of life. In a mate, he looks for security—both emotionally and financially, though his feelings of the heart will always win out over stock holdings. He also wants a woman whom he can greatly respect, one he'll be proud to call his.

Cancers, early on in life, can have many flings and adventures. They're curious and experimental many times—they like to try it all out. A less evolved Cancer may settle down too soon for fear of being alone. More mature Cancers usually wait for "the one" and live very happy, fulfilled lives. Many times Cancer can be quite faithful (though Cancer men are less so), though if she feels she's not with her future hubby, she won't think twice about cheating or dating two, even three other guys at once.

 ALERT!

A mature Cancer will find his place in the world and know just how to cope with happenings around him. A less evolved Cancer, though, will try to make the world adapt to him—all the while incorporating sneaky, deceptive maneuvers in order to "help" things along into place.

He/She: The Little Stuff Counts

Cancer woman is impressed with worldly men, but she also likes her men to be simple in some way. She's attracted to men who calm her and who are generally tranquil. She'll go for a man who looks great in jeans but who also cleans up well at a moment's notice—should she have to present him to the Queen. She likes a man who's sexy from the inside out, one who's discreet, not a poser, and certainly regal to those looking on him from the outside.

Cancer man also goes for sexy. Secretly, or for short periods of time, he may have relations with women who dress on the more suggestive side. Though he doesn't always admit it, Cancer man likes to be shocked and challenged. However, this is not usually the woman he chooses to marry. The woman who is to be Cancer man's partner for life will almost certainly be the one he can take home and present to Mama—a "good girl."

 ESSENTIAL

> Although Cancer man likes a woman to be sexy and sexed-up, he also wants a sweet, quiet woman as his life partner. Winning a Cancer man's heart indubitably requires a delicate balance on shaky ground.

Pillow Talk: Signs in the Bedroom

A Cancer will never directly say he wants to go to bed. He'll hint and maybe even joke about it, but then he'll claim he was just kidding—even when he wasn't. If he's joking about it with you, chances are he'd jump at the chance if offered to him. Cancers like sex—or rather, they like passionate sex. They feel their way through it. And they're versatile. One day, they'll want to go on for hours and the next be happy with a quick encounter. Let's talk about some of the differences between Cancer man and woman in love and bed.

The Secret Cancer Man

The Cancer man is a little confusing. He flirts continuously, never seeming to get enough of women—in fact, he doesn't know what he wants. But in truth, when Cancer man gets hold of his moods and grows up, he can be a wonderful mate. He's a great lover: attentive and sexual. If you want to have a fling with him, keep in mind that it may be short-lived. He'll show you all the attention in the world and make you feel like a goddess, but he probably won't call again. More likely, he'll show up at your door when he's been jilted by some current main squeeze. And once his self-confidence returns, he'll disappear again.

 QUESTION?

What's the one sure way to get a Crab man into bed?
Grab him. Cancer man will happily let himself be seduced by an aggressive woman. If he's unsure or dawdling about, the direct approach will work with him. Don't bother with words, just show him what you want with action.

The Secret Cancer Woman

Let Cancer woman talk, and show her that you really understand her. She's looking for a connection—however flimsy. She'll fill in the gaps. She tends to go for a he-man, whether that means macho, sexy, dominant, or noble. She's pretty flexible on dates. Though she can dress to the nines, she'd also be up for a hayride or a water amusement park date, for example. Cancer also loves to just hang out in front of the television. She's a complete lover of lighting candles about the house and giving or getting massages.

 ALERT!

If you give Cancer woman a sense of sexy and comforted at the same time, you'll have a great chance of seducing her all the way into your lair. Cook for her, and she may marry you tomorrow.

Almost all Cancer women are also open-minded and New-Age oriented in some way. Seduce her by showing her you like the same spiritual books she likes or that you at least appreciate what she's interested in. She'll like you more for it. Cancer woman can also be touchy-feely, and she likes big hugs and two strong arms to make her feel protected.

Sun Love Matches

Once again, Cancer can be idealistic. He's looking for the white picket fence and all the trimmings—a perfect wife, mother, lover, cook, and domestic live-in who will be affectionate with him always. Cancer simply doesn't like to fight. If he's involved with a person with many planets in Fire, he may choose to run instead. Also, he feels his way through the world, so an Air sign, or someone who rationalizes too much and bursts his idealistic bubble, will not be the one to capture his heart. Read on to learn about the love compatibility pairs with the female Crab.

Cancer Man

These two are both romantic, and they know how to give the other the emotional support each craves. Though they tend to be possessive with each other, the problems incurred seem to cancel each other out. In other words, these two mix well. In bed, they have the same style, though both secretly would like to dominate. To others, they appear to be soul mates. If one of the two doesn't have too much Air or Earth, this can be a very passionate, dramatic relationship. Should they find a way to be honest in their love and to trust each other deeply, this can be a probable long-term relationship, with a good chance for marriage.

Leo Man

No other sign in the zodiac knows how to give a good compliment like Cancer woman—and Leo man just eats this up. She's deep and emotional, and he finds that strangely affecting. She understands him and lets him know it. But he's actually not sure if he can trust her. He doesn't quite get her pulling back from him—and when she does it, he does it too. This can be confusing to both. But when Leo man gets insecure about the relationship, Cancer knows just how to come back and make him feel good again. In bed, Leo man is able to open Cancer up and make her purr. This can be a possible long-term partnership and a possible marriage.

 ESSENTIAL

Cancer and Leo can bring out the best in one another, as long as Cancer is honest about her feelings without getting too emotional. This way, Leo still has room to breathe.

Virgo Man

Cancer woman tolerates Virgo man to a point. But she wants more romance from him—more candlelight, more music, more wine, and a clearer demonstration of feelings. She knows he's crazy about her. Why doesn't he show it more? And why does he have to analyze every point? In fact, he repeats himself. Cancer gets the feeling he does it just to hear himself talk. Though she's able to soothe his ego, she sometimes gets annoyed when he's critical or judgmental, and at these times she's not liable to feel like giving him that extra attention. Cancer and Virgo both like sex, though Cancer wishes he would admit it and give in to his base desires. She sometimes wonders if Virgo is really in the moment or somewhere else. If Virgo can open up to Cancer woman, this can be a possible long-term relationship, though it's not a probable marriage.

 FACT

> Cancers have incredible influence over the general public. How they choose to use this power is up to them. Famous Crabs with this kind of charisma include Princess Diana, the Dalai Lama, P. T. Barnum, Ross Perot, Nancy Reagan, Frida Kahlo, and John Quincy Adams.

Libra Man

When they actually get around to talking about the rapport they have together, Libra and Cancer find they have a lot in common. Unfortunately, the two keep beating around the bush, and the problems can mount when they're both purposely avoiding confrontation. Cancer senses when Libra is unhappy, and the two can really affect each other, producing strange and powerful up-and-down mood swings. Instinctively, Cancer woman knows how to stroke Libra's libido. He sees her as the perfect woman and mother figure. In bed, Libra may seem a bit distant for Cancer. One time he's a passionate whirlwind. and the next he's as cold as an iceberg.

Cancer wishes she could repair the sometimes-dark side of Libra's soul and make him think more idealistically and less rationally. This drives her crazy. If Libra can feel a little more, this can be a possible long-term relationship, but it is not a probable marriage.

Scorpio Man

This may be the best combination for Cancer woman. If she can overlook his political views and deal with his stress periods from work, the two can be a match made in heaven. Sexually, dark Scorpio will subtly convince Cancer to take charge. She'll do it with gusto and the two of them in bed find exactly what they're looking for. These two are also incredibly dramatic. Scorpio wants Cancer to prove she's trustworthy. Cancer is able to do that once she sees she can trust him. This is a probable long-term relationship with an excellent chance for marriage as well.

 ESSENTIAL

Though Cancer is a bit more outgoing than Scorpio man, both are more than content to stay home, just the two of them, eating, watching television, or making love all evening.

Sagittarius Man

This is a classic case of opposites that really do attract. Sagittarius man is very different from Cancer woman, yet they seem to be good for each other. In fact, Sagittarius man is able to give Cancer woman a good boost of energetic power. She'll love the outings and adventures he takes her on. She's fascinated and warmed by the fact that he's so good at everything he does. And Sagittarius thinks Cancer woman is great; he respects her. Cancer woman finds in bed a sexual partner who can please her and make her feel loved. If Sagittarius can be faithful and let Cancer woman rule his domain, this can be a very possible long-term relationship, with a good chance for marriage.

 FACT

> When you think of Sagittarius men, think "different." Woody Allen, Mark Twain, Steven Spielberg, Beethoven, and Walt Disney are good examples of the Archer's famous imagination.

Capricorn Man

Cancer woman finds Capricorn man a stickler for so many things. Why can't he loosen up a little? In truth, either the two will see life completely through rose-colored glasses, or Capricorn will simply burst Cancer's romantic, visionary bubble (depending on Capricorn's other signs). Thank goodness he's faithful. Cancer loves this about him and also that he can be a rock for her— one she knows she can always lean on. Unfortunately, bed and sexuality may be a bit of a problem. Capricorn can be more practical than Cancer. If he can open up a little, he may just be able to tap into her hidden sensual, sexual energies. If Capricorn can learn to lighten up a little, these two can find a possible long-term thing together. Still, they are not a probable marriage.

Aquarius Man

Cancer woman is intrigued by Aquarius man. He's sexy, and he's out there. Together, these two can become wanderlust bohemians. He brings out her spiritual side. They're also both incredibly intuitive. However, both can be deceptive—especially Cancer woman when she wants to be. This bothers Aquarius, who sees himself as straightforward. Then again, he's able to wait out Cancer's push-and-pull techniques. Aquarius, in bed, likes it rougher than Cancer. Instead, she wonders if he's able to stay with her and only her. These two excite each other mentally, though, and they really can talk the night through about every subject in the world. This could be a possible long-term relationship, and a possible marriage beyond that.

Pisces Man

Pisces man intrigues Cancer woman. She has all the time in the world to get to know him and will give her best effort in doing so. Romantically and emotionally, the Fish is perfect for the Crab. The only problem here can be with "push-pull" on both parts—when angry, she crawls and he swims away. Also, Pisces man may or may not be the financial breadwinner Cancer hopes for. However, this doesn't make much difference. Cancer is wowed by Pisces' intuition and creativity. Soft, slow, romantic, and passionate sex heats up the rapport in bed. If Pisces can give in to Cancer's nurturing instinct, this can be a probable long-term relationship with a good chance for marriage.

 ESSENTIAL

> Both Cancer woman and Pisces man see things the same way and work to create a perfect home atmosphere. Probably, they both want children.

Aries Man

Aries man conquers Cancer's heart. He woos her, makes her feel special, and spoils her. Predictably, she gets hooked on the Ram. Even when he begins looking around at others, she tries to turn a blind eye to his flirtatious side. In bed, he knows how to tap into her creative energies. Lovemaking becomes a wild ride for both of them—adventurous, passionate, and even a little kinky. Aries man also loves when Cancer dotes on him. If she's strong enough to let him wander off with friends into his social habitat, he'll always come back to her. But this takes a lot of will power for Cancer woman. If she can do it, this can be a possible long-term thing, with marriage possible.

Taurus Man

With Taurus, Cancer knows she'll be taken care of. She relies on him and likes the feeling of security he gives her. She doesn't expect him to be unfaithful—and, most likely, he won't be. Cancer is much wiser than Taurus in the way of people and the world. Even so, he absolutely won't listen to her advice, and it gets him into a lot of trouble. In bed, Taurus has all the sensual moves Cancer craves. However, she may be a bit shy with him in the beginning—he wishes she'd just tell him what she wants. If the two can let go of emotional doubts and fears of the past, this can be a possible long-term relationship. It's also a possible marriage (but not a likely one).

 FACT

As far as what the Bull is looking for in a wife and mother, Cancer woman fits the old-fashioned bill perfectly. Unfortunately, the games between them mount up if they're not careful. Both move at a slow pace and are given to sidestepping conflict.

Gemini Man

Both are open-minded, curious, and outgoing. Though this is always true of Gemini, Cancer is only bubbly when she feels like it. Many times, in fact, Cancer would prefer a quiet candlelit dinner at home, while Gemini has other plans. He wants to go out and show off his lady love to others. Also, Gemini tells fibs here and there. Cancer, though, knows just how to play him right—if there's anyone who can get him to confess, it's the Crab. Creatively, these two spur each other on. In bed, their styles vary greatly, and Gemini would prefer to go faster and change positions more frequently. To Cancer, this starts feeling like sexual gymnastics—all the moves and none of the emotions. If Gemini man has some Water or a lot of Fire in his chart, this combo may work. If not, this is a possible long-term thing, but it's not a probable marriage.

 QUESTION?

> **What do you get when you combine a Gemini and Cancer together?**
> You get a Gemini/Cancer cusp. Here you have Air and Water, thinking and feeling, mutable and cardinal signs. People with this cusp include Meryl Streep, Errol Flynn, Jean-Paul Sartre, and Cyndi Lauper.

Love Planets: Venus and Mercury

Cancer in anyone's chart—even those with mostly all Fire or all Air, for example—will always enjoy dinners at home and long for a nice family life. Though his other signs may fight with this part of him, romantic notions will always creep into the psyche of a person with

Cancer influence. Below are the side effects you can expect with Cancer in your personal chart.

Venus in Cancer

Even if you have Air and Fire throughout your chart, Venus in Cancer will always make you a bit idealistic in love. You long for romance, and you dream of being swept away by passion and desire. A mate perfect for you would have to match your main influences. If you're mostly Water, look for the same in other people. Venus in Cancer can also conflict with your other signs. For instance, if you're a Sagittarius or an Aries, this Cancer aspect will fight with your need to travel and be out and about. You'll find that later on in life, your need for stability will win out, and you'll settle down and get comfortable. Venus in Cancer pairs well with Venus in Scorpio, Pisces, Virgo, Taurus, Leo, and Cancer.

Mercury in Cancer

You're great at giving advice, but you wish people would listen to what you're saying. Because you're not as pushy as Gemini (also a great advice-giver), others don't take in and reflect on your words of wisdom as much as they should. You're instinctive and know how to get confessions out of people—making them talk about things they wouldn't normally. You sincerely care about people and are uncannily adept at giving the perfect compliment. Mercury in Cancer goes well with Mercury in Pisces, Scorpio, Cancer, Gemini, Aquarius, and Taurus.

Chapter 5
Leo

Leo has such presence that he lights up a room and forces everyone to look his way. He also has the sunniest disposition of all the signs of the zodiac . . . when he feels like it. Just remember that lions occasionally do roar. And when he does, it's best to get out of his way. In this chapter, find out what makes Leo the powerful, dramatic soul he is.

The Generous Lion

There's almost no one as generous as Leo the Lion. In fact, she's much more comfortable giving than getting. The Lion will also spend when she has the chance, buying gifts for herself and for others without waiting for a holiday or any specific reason. Returning the favor with a gift will be nice for Leo, and she'll probably adore you for it. However, the one thing she wants more than anything is your appreciation and devotion. She needs to be respected and admired. In fact, she'll gravitate toward you if you can give her this without ceremony.

 FACT

In love, Leo wants someone as giving as she is. This is where many astrologers get it wrong. Financial gifts work up to a point, it's true, but Leo looks for an emotional connection more than anything. She longs to be persuaded and to be treated like she's the only woman on earth.

Though Leo is all Fire, she feels deeply. She instinctively knows who really cares about her and who doesn't—though she tends to project her feelings on others at times. This means that if she doesn't like someone, she'll immediately think the person doesn't like her either. No matter—Leo goes by a sense of skin. If another rubs her the wrong way, she'll simply turn away and reject the friendship or love situation. Once you've gotten on the bad side of Leo, too, there's not much you can do to win her over again. She'll forgive you, but she'll never forget. Damage control may simply be too difficult to be possible.

Queenly/Kingly Behavior

Like Pisces, Leo always has a sophisticated air about him. He can rise from humble beginnings, but he'll always find a way to come out on top. He's regal, and some believe he's even pretentious. Also, Leo doesn't particularly like to conform. He'll try a situation out, but if it's not to his liking, he won't hesitate to quickly move away from it.

 ALERT!

Leo can be your best friend or love mate. Though he's never out to hurt anyone, he'll talk behind your back or betray you if he believes you're not real with him! With Leo it's all or nothing: You're either with him or against him.

Even so, Leo is the best friend you can have. If she's a real friend, she'll be completely devoted to you. She'll keep all your secrets. She'll shower you with attention and affection. She'll be your champion in love. Although she's faithful, she won't be true to you for one minute if she thinks you're full of it. In other words, if she doubts your loyalty or your love, she won't resist sticking it to you when she can.

The Art of Attraction

Leo will always root for the underdog. She deeply empathizes with the one she believes to be in the right and will fight tooth and nail for him (like Aquarius, except that Leo is less naive). She always assesses the situation first and then takes action. Sometimes she can be apathetic, but if the person is a true friend, she'll do everything she can to help.

Above all, Leo despises pettiness in others. If she sees that someone is fixed on trivial things—too focused on details, a penny-pincher, unkind, or unfriendly toward the less fortunate—she'll lose her cool. Signs of the zodiac who pick a fight for no reason or who have some of these traits will never win a Leo's heart. Leo is always a noble creature, and she expects those around her to be as well.

The Long Haul

Pride is a genuine factor when considering a Leo as a future mate. Ego is essential to a Lion. Many think that Leo is cocky and full of himself, but this isn't usually so. Instead, Leo is insecure and worries that people won't recognize him as powerful. In fact, keeping a Lion happy almost always has to do with stroking his ego the right way. If he's constantly made jealous or treated badly, he'll keep with the relationship for only enough time to see if he can turn things around—Leo's an optimist at heart. But if he can't take the heat any longer, he'll sprint off to find cooler waters.

 FACT

> Leos let pride determine who their partners will be. They want someone who's faithful and loving, someone who will tell them how wonderful they are at all times. An insecure Leo is not a pretty sight.

However, Leo can't stand those who fawn all over him. He wants a partner with a real spine who can stand up to him and to take control. Yes, Leo is strong. You'd think he wanted a mate to carry out his every whim. Not so. He does want someone who will go along with him, but he also needs a partner who will put him in his place if need be. More than anything, Leo needs to respect a partner intensely. Without the grand respect, Leo can fall into lust but never in love.

He/She: The Little Stuff Counts

To lose a Leo fast, dress scruffily or show up at her doorstep unkempt. Leo will take you to a little hole in the wall because she doesn't want to be seen with you. Appearance is important to Leo, whether man or woman. Leo takes great care while dressing for a date, and she expects you to do the same. Hair is very important to Leos. For a Leo man, a woman with long, beautiful hair is a fantastic turn-on. Compliment a Leo woman on her eyes and/or her hair, and she'll be yours for the evening.

Leo always goes for sexy. A man with an earring won't turn a Leo woman off—if it's tasteful. However, she will find excessive jewelry on a man too much. Contrary to popular belief, Leo does not like ostentatious showoffs. The male Lion goes for sexy and subtle. Remember, too, that Leo likes to feel he's won someone over with his charm and intelligence. If Leo's date starts checking out other guys while she's on his arm, he'll play it cool, but he'll also take away all her Brownie points. You won't win by making Leo angry.

 ALERT!

Though Leo can hold his own in any verbal war, he'll blame you for making him lose his cool. He doesn't like to fight and won't stay long with a partner who reduces him to it.

Though Leo doesn't like to fight, she does like challenge. If she wins a partner too easily, she'll wonder why. Cocky as she may seem, though, she'll never think, "Oh, I conquered him right away because I'm wonderful." Gemini might say this, but Leo won't. Also remember that Leo goes by feeling and instinct more than by rationalization. She's all Fire and wants to be swept away with love and desire.

Pillow Talk: Signs in the Bedroom

Leo is lusty and loves sex. Leo longs to be won over, body and soul. A little playfulness in the bedroom helps the Lion feel more relaxed. Like a cat, people of this sign can be curious, too, about all kinds of bed play. Though she'll shy away from sex toys—perhaps indicating to you that she thinks they're vulgar—this may be all for show. Secretly, she'll hope you can find just the right way to persuade her into trying them. Leo can also go back and forth in terms of her willingness to try other new things. This seriously depends on her partner. If she feels completely respected and adored, she's more likely to let loose. If not, she's unlikely to feel very adventurous—ever.

 ESSENTIAL

> Leo is a romantic at heart and must decide beforehand if a partner is just a sex mate or a more long-term thing. She's capable of having a fling if she's convinced it won't hurt anyone—especially herself.

The Secret Leo Man

It has been said that Leos are not as strong and sturdy as they seem. This is sometimes doubly true of the male Lion. Always remember that narcissism is a product of deep insecurity. He appears to be sleek, cool, and graceful. He speaks through movements rather than through words—a smile, a shake of the head, a wink, or a touch. If he talks a lot, he's covering a silence that, to him, is unbearable—he more clearly hears the thoughts in his head. Leo men are notoriously critical of themselves.

Sarcastic Barbs

Both Sagittarius and Leo men are also known for their sarcastic barbs. Their little subtle comments are designed to put you off guard and off balance. Again, this comes from a need to reduce others. Unfortunately, this is sometimes the ruse they use to simply feel better about themselves. Your only good counter against this is to reply with a mature, noble answer. If you use sarcasm or nastiness back, ironically enough, Leo will feel like you're the one attacking *him*.

 FACT

A more evolved Leo won't use sarcasm to belittle you. If you know a Leo who does, don't reduce yourself to his level. He won't respect you for it. Instead, give him an ultimatum. If he feels he'll lose you because of his insensitivity, he'll quickly change his ways.

The King of the Bedroom

One important thing to remember is that Leo man absolutely must dominate in bed. If you're aggressive with him, he won't like it. He needs to feel like a real he-man. This is essential to him. The coyer you are, the better. Sexually, Leo man also needs to feel loved and nurtured. He likes being "mommied." He runs hot and cold, though. If he's feeling like he loves you in the moment, he's a dynamo who puts Rudolph Valentino's romantic repertoire to shame. If he doesn't, you may get the feeling a tornado has just hit you.

A Sensitive Soul

Leo man is sensitive, too. If you insult him about his lovemaking, he won't defend himself and try to make it better (the way Aries would). And he certainly won't let it roll off his back easily (as Sagittarius does). Instead, he'll instinctively get a bad feeling about you without consciously knowing where it came from. He'll push you away. Then he'll look elsewhere for a partner who makes him feel good about himself.

The Secret Leo Woman

She also appears strong, but she's got barriers up. Deep down, she doesn't realize that she has awesome power. Once she taps into this, it's smooth sailing. Again, a Leo woman can be insecure, too. Her need for compliments is unusually insatiable. But they better be real or Leo will sense it. Unlike Leo man, a Leo woman needs to be dominated completely. She's good at being aggressive and taking charge in bed, but she doesn't really like it. Instead, she wants deep, powerful, mysterious sex. Sex is the only place she's convinced herself she can let down her guard. She wants to surrender to a mate—even if she finds him difficult to come by.

Leos, like Virgos, are very selective about their friends and mates. Virgo, though, will sometimes give more of a chance than Leo will—even though Virgo trusts less.

 ALERT!

> Leo woman has constant scripts and scenarios running in her head. If you can say just the right words or touch her in just the right place, she'll be yours. She may even feel that your connection with her is destiny.

Oh, and here's one more thing: Don't ever try to manipulate a Leo woman, in or out of bed. Leo woman may come off as a femme fatale, but that's because she chooses to be seen that way. It's a defense mechanism. She may like to play and provoke, but she's almost never sneaky or deceptive like Gemini or Scorpio. And she'll hate it if you think that she is. Instead, if a Leo woman is reserved and doesn't speak up about something bothering her, either ask her what's wrong or let it pass. Don't immediately assume that Leo is formulating some scheme against you. She isn't. Deep down, Leo's good. Treat her like the nobility she is, and you'll always win with the female Lion.

Sun Love Matches

Leo woman always looks for a mate who excites her. She hates being bored (just like Aries woman). In fact, she sometimes gets into trouble because she has a habit of going for dangerous, dark souls whom she believes she can rescue and bring to the light. In this way, she's attracted to Scorpio, Capricorn, and Taurus men—though these matches don't usually last. Leo man, on the other hand, may want excitement, but he also intensely craves security and a mother figure. He wants a mate who he knows will take good care of his future brood. Only a mature Leo man will be faithful, but he always expects it of his partner. Once again, jealousy is not the way to win any Leo's heart.

 FACT

> Many Leo men, by the way, also have a hidden desire to produce a male offspring. This is just something he instinctively wishes for from childhood to maturity.

Keep in mind that Leo man is not necessarily looking for the same things in a mate as Leo woman. (See individual signs to learn more about pairings with Leo man.) Read on to learn about love matches with Leo woman.

Leo Man

Normally, two signs together make a perfect match, but not so with two Leos. Male and female Lions require so much attention and adoration that satisfaction in this pairing is nearly impossible. It's an especially precarious balance to achieve between two people striving for the same goal. In bed, Leo man's hot-and-cold streaks drive Leo woman crazy—for good or for bad. This match purely depends on the type of Leo you're dealing with.

If the two are mature, this can be a possible long-term relationship, even a possible marriage.

 ESSENTIAL

> A Leo-Leo coupling strongly depends on how evolved the people are. If both or even just one is mature, it can be a wonderful love. Two young, inexperienced Leos, though, have absolutely no chance together. They're constantly competing.

Virgo Man

This is, perhaps, the worst choice for a Leo woman. As a friend, these two go wonderfully together. They both like the finer things in life, and Virgo can be generous with Leo woman. Leo also loves the way Virgo can judge people. Secretly, she does it too. Though Virgo is freer with his trust, he's able to find a good balance in naming friends and foes. In bed, however, Virgo doesn't normally open up enough for Leo woman. And when he gets nitpicky and starts dissecting situations and people, Leo goes insane. This man is too mentally heavy for Leo, who wants excitement but also tranquility. This is not a probable long-term relationship, and it's not a likely marriage either.

Libra Man

Like Leo, Libra loves beautiful settings. He fascinates Leo woman. They're both trying to figure each other out. Leo doesn't necessarily trust Libra, but she loves his charm, his sexy ways, and his wit. Libra can be distant in bed, but when he's really there, Leo woman is completely taken by him. It's just too bad that he thinks she wants to lead. Deep down, she hopes he'll rise up to the challenge and dominate her more. This is a possible long-term relationship, but it's not a probable marriage.

 FACT

> Leo scares Libra man too much to be a choice for a long-term mate. He sees her as a risk, a femme fatale out to break him. He keeps weighing the odds of being with her. He's sometimes critical with her, though she handles it well.

Scorpio Man

Leo's convinced she's not in love with him. Then, out of nowhere, she falls. How did that happen? Perhaps she was busy keeping up with his moods. His self-pity drives her crazy, but she loves the idea of rescuing him from his dark side. She loves all his mystery, in fact. If she had to pinpoint when she first had real feelings for him, she'll realize it was when she finally went to bed with him. To her, he's the perfect lover—sensual, sexual, and intense. In the bedroom, these two are a match made in heaven. Out of the bedroom, however, they have all kinds of quarrels and misunderstandings. This is a very probable long-term thing, but it's not a recommended marriage (although this really depends on the other planets in Scorpio's chart).

Sagittarius Man

There are two kinds of Sagittarius men—the dark, pensive kind who only talks when he has something to say, and the happy-go-lucky puppy-dog variety. Leo is attracted to the first. There's something dangerous about him. She fears she has to tiptoe around him and will walk a fine line to keep him from going off the deep end. But she puts up with it. Why? He's one of the most intelligent men around. She respects him. He's adventurous, take-charge, and macho. He's one of the only men she'll allow to dominate her.

 ALERT!

It's not common but it happens sometimes . . . Sagittarius men can have a violent nature. Like Gemini women, it's innate. Be careful! A Leo woman will sometimes tolerate emotional abuse but never physical.

And in the bedroom? He's a stallion! A Casanova! Incredible! He excites her like no one else (except maybe Scorpio). If Leo can control herself, and if she doesn't get too aggressive or dramatic with the male Archer (who despises scenes, private or public), this can be a probable long-term relationship and a very possible marriage.

Capricorn Man

Capricorn man can sometimes be a bit dull for sunny Leo woman. But if he's not jaded and still has a bit of the wonder he's naturally born with, these two can play and laugh. She loves his sense of humor. He also gives her a sense of security that she finds very attractive. Sometimes, though, he gets too close for comfort. He understands her (perhaps a little too much), and this can spell trouble. He analyzes her and criticizes her. She protects herself by pretending he doesn't have it right, though she knows deep down that he's right on the money. In bed, sparks don't fly the way she hopes. Capricorn man holds back. He's got secrets and all kinds of issues, she thinks. She may or may not be correct in this assumption. If Capricorn can ease up a little, this can be a possible long-term partnership and a possible marriage beyond that.

Aquarius Man

In the beginning, Aquarius is so easy to be with. He's the male best friend she never had. She's amazed by his social skills and his natural ability to communicate and tell a good story. She thinks she's found The One. But then the problems start. She gets annoyed and even jealous when all his buddies run to him when they need cheering up. And he always drops her to help them. Sexually, their partnership is wonderful, but she feels there's something missing. She just can't put her finger on what that is. Aquarius thinks Leo is a bit too sensitive. Why can't she lighten up? If Aquarius uses his instincts more with Leo and is careful with her feelings, this can be a possible long-term thing, but it's still not a probable marriage.

Pisces Man

Pisces man can get immediately obsessed with Leo woman if he doesn't conquer her fully. She loves the look in his eyes and his deep analyses of the people around them. Pisces also adores Leo's sense of humor and her zest for life. If Leo has one or two Water signs in her chart, Pisces can be good for her. He actually brings out the best in her. He knows just how to play her and can cheer her up on a moment's notice.

 FACT

> You can sometimes spot Pisces men by their one common attribute: beautiful eyes, light or soft brown in color. They usually have a deep, sad look about them that makes Pisces seem pensive.

Though Pisces is a trustworthy soul, Leo sometimes doesn't know what to make of him. She needs to know him better before she can trust him. Once she does, she sees that he is definitely worthy of her. Pisces, too, is able to adjust to his surroundings the same way Leo can. He's got an innate sense of refinement and style. She wishes he would stop pulling away, getting quiet when things get tough. She takes charge. If Leo doesn't feel that Pisces manipulates her too much, this can be a probable long-term thing and even a possible marriage.

Aries Man

Aries man gets Leo excited, and she wonders where he gets all his energy. In the beginning, it seems as if they really "get" each other. They admire each other's sense of style and way of handling things. Aries also inspires Leo's creativity and a compliment from him goes a long way for the Lioness. However, Aries' attention is sometimes sporadic, at best. It depends how mature he is. Leo will follow him around for a while, but then she'll want to retreat into her cave—Aries will want to follow. If she lets him in, he can woo her easily. In bed, they can be a great match. Thank goodness Aries is a real man, she thinks. She also loves the fact that people look up to him. Together they know how to paint the town. If Aries remains interested in her and doesn't hurt Leo's hypersensitive ego, this couple can be a long-term thing. They may even make an excellent marriage.

Taurus Man

He seems almost like a Fire sign when she first meets him. He's charming and possibly even a bit dangerous. Leo's definitely attracted to him. There's one big problem: Taurus can be petty. He doesn't like the way she spends money. Either he lectures her incessantly about it, or he keeps quiet and withdraws from her without explaining why. He also makes her jealous by flirting with her friends. In bed, think heat, sensuality, passion, and intensity. He's got the perfect style for her—he can dominate her completely and still service her in all the ways she dreams. He won't stop until she's satiated. This can be an excellent long-term affair, but it is not a probable marriage.

 ESSENTIAL

> Taurus is old-fashioned. He wants to control the Lioness by telling her how she should act. It bothers him that she's so outgoing and nice to people, when he wants her just for himself.

Gemini Man

Leo woman thinks that Gemini man is amoral. She doesn't approve of the things he says and does. But Leo can't help herself. Gemini not only has a magnetic sense of innate sexiness, he makes her laugh like no one else can. He's street-smart, and she respects this about him. He knows how to deal with people in a way she could never dream of, and he's especially great with kids. He's so approachable and she feels comfortable with him. In fact, she loves spending alone time with him—too bad he always has fans waiting on the sidelines. Thank goodness Gemini man doesn't fight dirty like his female counterpart. Gemini man thinks the Lioness is all woman, and tries to show her so in bed. Leo, though, gets the feeling that sex is a sport to Gemini. And she's probably right. If Gemini has some Fire or Water in his chart, this can be a possible long-term thing. If so, it's even a possible marriage.

Cancer Man

These two connect in some strange way. Cancer man brings out Leo's nurturing instincts, and he's able to take care of her in return. Although the two make an odd match, their relationship can work in and out of the bedroom. She gets hooked on his ups and down, which can be exciting for her in a way that's not necessarily healthy.

 FACT

> Cancer man knows just the right thing to say to Leo woman and when to say it. She respects him though she's not sure if she should trust him. If he's sneaky or manipulative with her, he'll lose her immediately.

Making love, they can get adventurous together, and Cancer makes Leo feel things she didn't know she could. If Cancer is evolved, this can be a positive long-term relationship, and a very possible marriage beyond that.

Love Planets: Venus and Mercury

Leo is sunny, outgoing, protective, funny, and cool. Having a little Leo in your other planets is always a plus, with many more positive side effects than negative. First, check out your Venus and Mercury in Appendix C at the back of this book. Then read on. Leo also always adds a little luck to anyone's life. Leos are unusually blessed with good fortune.

Venus in Leo

A grand love is your absolute ideal. You like every-thing grand, in fact: big, sweet gestures and romantic moves. Though you may have suffered earlier on in life, you tend to be an optimist at heart. You either trust or you don't. When you do, you can be faithful and loyal to a fault. You're attracted to people who seem to need you. You like to be in control, but you want someone who can also dominate you or you won't fall in love. If you are a woman with Venus in Leo, you love sex and long to be completely seduced. A man with Venus in Leo wants to feel deeply but fears he won't. You go well with Venus in Leo, Pisces, Scorpio, Cancer, Sagittarius, and Aries.

Mercury in Leo

There is nothing that frustrates you more than a person who talks around and around the point without actually getting to it. It drives you nuts. You'll find some good excuse and be out the door before the talker can realize what's happened. You're direct with what you say, and you're good at grasping the situation for what it really is. Though you tend to be idealistic—you wish everyone would follow through on their claims and promises, the way you always do—you do forgive easily. You have a talent for accepting people for who they are. People also like talking with you, and they think you're pretty cool and crafty. Mercury in Leo goes well with Mercury in Aquarius, Gemini, Leo, Aries, Libra, and Sagittarius.

Chapter 6
Virgo

Sometimes you can predict what Virgo may do, but other times he'll surprise you. Many Virgos are born with built-in protective walls. They only let you see what they want you to see. Here, discover what's going on behind the tricky Virgo façade that goes something like, "I'm fine, you're fine, leave me alone . . . Where are you going?"

The Selective One

Virgo can shut himself off from the world, but most of the time he seems outgoing and friendly. Though his quick, funny comebacks aren't meant to hurt, these comments can sometimes be construed as sarcastic or biting. Don't read too much into it. Virgo is more likely to mock himself than to put the joke on you. In fact, a Virgo's worst enemy is usually himself. He has to be especially careful to treat himself well and not to wander down the path of self-pity. True, he bounces back quickly, and chances are good that you won't have time to see his super ego-sensitive side. He'll just disappear when he's angry. Also, Virgo is apt to keep his self-perceived faults under wraps.

Getting Through the Barrier

In fact, Virgo is only likely to fall in love with a person who can see past all her barriers and self-imposed walls. Though it is her dream to be uncovered, she'll never admit it. She's even less likely to let you in if she doesn't want to. In fact, she can be downright anti-social. You may find it frustrating when she calls it a night just when you're supposed to meet up with your friends.

Then again, if Virgo trusts you—really trusts you—you've won a true, reliable friend and lover. Though Virgo gives everyone a chance, it's not easy to win her real respect and loyalty. And there's no one who will be there for you like Virgo. She does everything necessary to get the job done. She's efficient, she's reliable, and she knows just the right thing to say to cheer you up. In fact, you'd think Virgo is a rock. Don't be fooled—she's strong, but she also suffers in silence. A less evolved Virgo almost always seems angry just below the surface. Be careful not to tap into this by arguing too much.

 ESSENTIAL

> Part of the reason Virgo is likely to fall into depression has to do with the way he keeps his emotions bottled up. When he finally releases them, it's like a torrential storm, unexpected and powerful.

A Battle Within

Virgo wavers between paranoia and excessive trust. Fortunately, she's bright, funny, witty, and refined. Like Scorpio and Leo, though, Virgo believes people are either with him or against him. But unlike Scorpio and Leo, who go more by a sense of skin, Virgo tries to rationalize things away. She can't help dissecting things. A less mature Virgo will analyze every move of her love partner, right down to the way he says, "Let's talk later."

Here's the rub: Virgo doesn't want you to know that she's a real softie. She loves love and wants to be smitten ten times over. But she can't shake the feeling that she needs to protect herself. She's more romantic than she likes to let on, simply because she can't bear the thought of being considered a fool.

Scared of Love?

Virgo is cursed with a fear of love. Many times, she even pushes prospective love mates away unwittingly because she's afraid of what a real love match might mean. She'd have to be open. Exposed. Vulnerable. This is Virgo's biggest hurdle. A younger, less evolved Virgo, unfortunately, is also likely to get involved with an emotional or physically abusive partner. Though almost all Virgos seem mature at a very young age, it usually takes awhile for a Virgo to truly grow emotionally. For this reason, many Virgos find their real love mates in their thirties, instead of in their twenties.

 ALERT!

Out of all the signs in the zodiac, don't get on the bad side of Virgo. Like Scorpio, Capricorn, or Gemini, she can get nasty or vengeful. Virgo won't completely forgive, and she certainly won't forget.

The Art of Attraction

Here's an important thing to remember. The only way to get a Virgo to truly fall in love with you is to make sure he knows he can depend on you. He needs to trust you. Plus, you cannot be a pushover. Virgo needs excitement on the scale of wildfire. You have to stimulate his senses as well as his brain. Virgo also loves to laugh. He has a great sense of humor, but there are few who can make him really laugh out loud. If you can, you've got an ace in the hole. Also remember that Virgo is an Earth sign and, not surprisingly, will also look for financial security.

The Long Haul

Virgo women have an instinctive nurturing side. They make great mothers because they know when to be affectionate and when to discipline. Though she tends to be a pushover with her kids—she spoils them—Virgo woman is not likely to be overshadowed or undermined by her mate. A good husband for Virgo is one who knows to leave the details of raising their progeny to her. She knows just the right way to do it, and he trusts her good sense. Instead, Virgo wants her partner to be there more for her. She needs the support only he can give her in order for her to run the family the way it should be.

 ESSENTIAL

Those thinking of taking Virgo as a mate should be aware that Virgo has a possessive side when it comes to family. She wants the control of the children, as well as the full attention of her husband. In other words, everyone must look to her for guidance.

He/She: The Little Stuff Counts

Virgo men and women both tend to be attracted to a subtle sexiness. They like refinement in a mate and can't stand showoffs. Instead, Virgo believes, sexiness should come from within. Virgo can look good in jeans or dressed up for a night on the town. A Virgo woman will notice the way her man dresses—and she'll expect him to suit up accordingly, depending on what they have planned. In other words, she'll expect him to dress well if they're supposed to meet the parents that day, but she'll be just as happy to see him in an old button-down and jeans for a long car trip. Just keep in mind that Virgo woman will notice and remember what you choose to wear.

 ALERT!

> Don't ever ask Virgo for advice unless you plan to use it and follow it! All Virgos take their time, and they put a lot of effort into an answer. If you ignore their counsel, they won't be likely to give you more suggestions in the future.

Virgo man isn't quite as picky about how his woman dresses. He'll be more interested, instead, in seeing whether she listens and respects what he says. All Virgos will be highly offended if a mate asks the same question two or three times. For a Virgo, words are very important. He'll listen closely to what you say, and he'll expect you to do the same for him.

Pillow Talk: Signs in the Bedroom

Virgo needs a strong mate who can stand up to her. Most Virgos are verbally powerful, and they expect the same of their partners. Virgo woman is likely to be attracted to men who can help her lighten up her outlook on life and herself. She's usually drawn to those who can lessen her load of responsibilities. Her life is tough enough; she wants her relationship to be problem-free. She despises arguing, but some people just rub her the wrong way. Also, both Virgo man and Virgo woman only go to bed with someone whom they feel respects and cares for them—more than just in a physical way.

The Secret Virgo Man

Here's a tip: Both Virgo men and women hate being a slave to their own passions, but they love sex. They just try not to admit it sometimes. For Virgo man (as for Virgo woman), sex is a process. He sometimes doesn't see a good thing even when it's standing in front of him. He's not a big romantic in the early stages. Things need to build for him. For a woman to grab his heart, she can't be too available to him, but she can't let him ignore her either—he'll pull away at a moment's notice. He'll test her, too, and see how much he can get away with.

Encouragement

Unlike a Virgo woman, a Virgo man is a bit unsure of his bedroom prowess. His woman should use words to restore his confidence. Then she should pull away a bit and let him work for her. With Virgo man, it's always push-pull. To seduce him into bed, a few well-placed words will tell him that you're interested.

The Secret Virgo Woman

On the other hand, a Virgo woman will be very influenced with hints here and there before the actual act. Make her think about what languorous, beautiful sex could be like and let that stew in her brain for awhile. Unfortunately, you won't necessarily know whether a Virgo woman is interested in you. She usually plays it cool and doesn't like to wear her heart on her sleeve. Similarly, if she cries or has an emotional outburst, it doesn't necessarily mean it concerns you. Get to the bottom of the situation, and you'll thank yourself later.

Sensual and Sexual

A Virgo woman is sensual and sexual. She loves having her hair stroked and her feet rubbed. She loves massages, too. Though she's as naughty as the rest of us, she likes creating a "good girl" image for those around her. Think "virgin." Ask a Virgo woman for anything showy or extra-kinky and—guaranteed—you will absolutely never see her again. She wants to be treated with respect and dignity, in and out of bed. Though she sometimes falls for the rogue, she really wants to be seduced with sweetness and purity at the heart of it all.

Sun Love Matches

Virgo can be a contradiction in terms. Though he longs for security, he sometimes goes for the truly unattainable.

Why? A less mature Virgo subconsciously seeks to punish himself and learn from the experience. He longs to understand the world and the way it works—shooting for the stars (or, on the negative side, choosing a mate who's completely wrong for him) seems to him to be all part of a bigger plan. He's also attracted to many different kinds of partners. Virgo can tend to stay in bad relationships longer than he should. Fortunately, a more mature Virgo is quite rational. When he finally finds the right partner—The One—he chooses wisely. As an Earth sign, Virgo pairs well with other Earth signs. He sometimes gets along well with Air and with other analytical signs, like Scorpio.

Read on to discover the love combinations for Virgo woman.

Virgo Man

When two Virgos get together, gone are the terms "compromise" and "middle ground." They either get along famously, or they're at each other's throats. True, a little bickering can sometimes be good foreplay. For them, though, when neither is willing to back down, a simply harmless argument can escalate into a full-blown fight. At the other end of the spectrum, Virgo man and woman instinctively understand each other. They usually know how to make each other happy. Once they start recounting their day or telling stories to each other, fun and laughter consume them. In bed, they let down their guards completely and can have "soul" sex—powerful, intense, and even a bit wild. All in all, this can be a good long-term relationship, with a very probable marriage ahead.

ESSENTIAL

> Virgo has a tendency to be antisocial. This actually works for her in a relationship. Together, Virgo man and woman can stay home or just spend quiet nights out somewhere at a little neighborhood place. Fortunately, their living styles are very similar.

Libra Man

Libra can be a heartbreaker for Virgo woman. He's dangerous for her. She tries not to let him fascinate her, but she just can't seem to help herself. He's got that sexiness within. She thinks she can win him over and make him faithful only to her. Maybe she can, but it's not easy. Libra man knows he can rile up Virgo woman. Sometimes he does it for fun, and other times he does it because he's not sure what he wants. This drives Virgo crazy. Though she should blame him for inconsistency, she usually blames herself. In bed, though, these two go together extremely well. If Libra dedicates himself to Virgo and gives up his Casanova ways, this can be a possible long-term thing, with marriage a possibility.

Scorpio Man

Virgo woman barely skims the surface in trying to get to know Scorpio man. She looks in the wrong places. In fact, she doesn't quite know how to deal with him. Virgo may just lose her mind trying to analyze

Scorpio's moods. She can't keep up with him. She's also more practical. Fortunately, both like to analyze, and gradually they find that they get along wonderfully. Their differences keep them bound and fascinated. These two can be good in bed together if Virgo lets down her emotional guard. Then he'll really make her knees weak. This can be a possible long-term relationship and maybe even a good marriage.

Sagittarius Man

Virgo woman intrigues Sagittarius man. She seems to know what she wants, and he likes that. They might even go away on a little weekend trek together. If so, that's when the problems start. Though Virgo is sexually attracted to the male Archer and she likes his style, she questions him a bit too much. And even though Virgo mostly just likes to play devil's advocate, Sagittarius can get easily offended when she doesn't take his words to heart.

 QUESTION?

What's the biggest downfall with Virgo and Sagittarius together?
Too many personal questions will make Sagittarius flee. Virgo wants to know about his past—she's curious. Sagittarius hates answering things about himself. Her curiosity is too much, too aggressive, too fast.

She also reduces him to little arguments (however small), and this bothers him. In bed, Virgo's in for a wild ride. He goes more by instinct, though, and she would prefer to hear how he feels from his own mouth. He speaks through silence and movements. This is a possible long-term relationship, but it's not a likely marriage.

Capricorn Man

Finally, Virgo woman has found a man who can ground her. Together they know the right way to get things done. Capricorn helps Virgo with her responsibilities and can come off like a father figure at times. Though Virgo can't stand the father act, she does respect Capricorn and believes what he says. Virgo instinctively trusts Capricorn, which she should. Capricorn man, though, is a little wary of Virgo woman. He senses her emotional capacity underneath it all, and it scares him. Also, he knows he'll have a tough time controlling her. In bed, these two make a sizzling match. If Virgo woman can let the Goat tell her what to do— and if she manages to listen—they can make a very good long-term partnership. They have an excellent chance for marriage as well.

Aquarius Man

These two get along really well. Virgo and Aquarius make each other laugh, and Aquarius has enough of a laid-back attitude to make Virgo feel at ease. Though Virgo doesn't know whether or not she should rely on

Aquarius man, she believes she can. This may or may not be true. But Aquarius doesn't have any hidden agendas. In fact, Aquarius will get annoyed if Virgo doubts his true intentions (even if they're not good ones). In bed, Aquarius is the first to really open up Virgo. They can get pretty creative between the sheets. If Virgo doesn't get too serious with Aquarius right away, this can be a probable long-term thing. It's also a very possible marriage.

Pisces Man

Pisces man has a quiet strength that Virgo woman admires. She likes his odd and quirky sense of humor and knows he's intelligent. This time, though, it's Pisces man who's not sure if he can trust Virgo woman. He sees her spinning her wheels and wonders why she lets the little things bother her. He's famous for seeing the "big picture." Though he tries desperately to help her come to the same conclusions, these two always seem to wind up on separate pages.

 ESSENTIAL

Pisces man always has a kind of otherworldly sense about him. He's born with wisdom beyond his years. Though Virgo appreciates this, she doesn't quite understand why. She winds up telling him what to do. Instead, she should listen to him more carefully.

Also, they move at two different rates in the relationship. Virgo may be ready to go to bed before he is. When they make it there, their mating will be slow and sensual. Virgo may want more of a warrior type in bed than the sensual Pisces. This match is not a good bet for the long term, and it's not a probable marriage.

Aries Man

Virgo woman amuses Aries man—in a good way. He backs her up in her little tiffs with this person and that. Though he picks his fights more carefully, he admires her nevertheless for standing up for herself. In the beginning, Aries man makes Virgo think she's found the love of a lifetime. He's romantic and passionate, and she can actually feel herself falling—but too late. By the time she's hooked for real, he may be on to his next conquest. It depends how mature he is, and if he's able to give Virgo time to open up and let him really know her. If Virgo can go in with the right frame of mind, and Aries is serious about giving her a chance, this can be a possible long-term relationship. It's also a possible marriage, though not a probable one.

Taurus Man

Many times Virgo woman is Taurus man's ideal. Though she's not as old-fashioned as she seems, she passes as the kind of gal Taurus man wants to marry. The only problem is that Taurus man hates confrontation of any kind. When Virgo woman wants a straight answer, he runs away. If she lets the issue go, he'll come back to her with a response in due time. If she persists, he'll label her as a troublemaker and go off in search of greener, more tranquil pastures. However, if the two can be sensitive with each other's feelings, this can be a probable long-term thing. They also have a good chance for marriage.

 ALERT!

> When they go out, Virgo loves the fact that Taurus is generous. And if there's anyone who can get Virgo going in bed, it's the Bull. Sexually, they work.

Gemini Man

These two can get into tons of mischief together—they actually egg each other on. They make each other laugh. Gemini man likes to rely on Virgo woman. Unfortunately, Virgo woman can be more sensitive than Gemini man. This can get in the way of their communication. In fact, the two sometimes misunderstand each other terribly. Gemini makes Virgo paranoid, and Virgo weighs Gemini down. Gemini also needs to do what he says. If he doesn't, Virgo is going to wonder if Gemini is actually even more flighty than he seems to be. Virgo doesn't necessarily trust him. In bed, they can have fun if Gemini can prove it's not just a fling, or if Virgo concedes that it is just that. This can be a possible long-term relationship, but it's not a probable marriage.

Cancer Man

Cancer man brings out Virgo's emotional side. Though he can appear to be superficial, which Virgo never is, she forgives him and gets to know his deeper side over time. Virgo, however, is stronger than Cancer man—or she appears to be. If she can let down her strong (sometimes harsh) exterior, these two could get along. But since Cancer operates on a different spiritual level than Virgo, they may never click into place. In bed, the two can experiment and find new sexual adventures. But that's only if Virgo can be more subtle in her approach. Also, Cancer shies away from conflict. They may find a very precarious middle ground, so this can be a possible long-term thing but not a probable marriage.

 FACT

Virgo is more direct than the sidestepping Crab. He likes to avoid heavy conversations as much as Virgo likes to have it straight. Unfortunately, these two have completely different ways of dealing with life.

Leo Man

Leo woman and Virgo man have almost no chance together. How about Virgo woman with Leo man? Maybe. She knows how to give a good compliment, and Leo man knows he can rely on her when he needs her. Though he sees the way she looks at things as narrow-minded at times, she also admires him for his wit and smarts. Leo tries hard to get passionate with her, but can't make up his mind if she's the love of his life or someone who will lead to his downfall. He wishes they could always get along, and he finds her methods of communication a little hard. Sexually they can go well together as long as Virgo lets Leo man lead. This is a possible long-term relationship, but it's not a likely marriage.

Love Planets: Venus and Mercury

A little Virgo in your chart will make it easier for you to understand the motives of other people. It may make you a bit abrasive—you could stand to soften your ideals and outlook somewhat—but it will also give you insight into the human condition. A certain critical nature enters the picture here, too—one that you turn on yourself and on others. With Virgo in any star or planet, you should be aware of being too hard on yourself. If you're not kind and forgiving with you, who else will be? Here, discover the intricacies of Virgo in your chart.

 ESSENTIAL

Venus in Virgo has a tendency to let moods affect her. When she's happy, she jokes, laughs, and is easy to get along with. When she's not, she can pick fights or argue just for the sake of it.

Venus in Virgo

Love is important to you even though you spend more time alone than you'd like. With you, love is all or nothing. Security is also important to you. True, you stay in a doomed relationship longer than you should, but you don't have any delusions. You know whether it's going to work. Where you have sex is actually very important to you. First, you like to decide where it is you're going to consummate—your place, his, or elsewhere. Venus in Virgo is paired well with Venus in Capricorn, Virgo, Taurus, Aquarius, Libra, Gemini, and Pisces.

Mercury in Virgo

You're self-critical and wish you weren't. You also tend to be paranoid about what others think of you. Mercury in Virgo, though, helps you to analyze those around you. It's a wonderful sign for those who write, study, or are interested in music. You remember conversations and lyrics to songs you only heard once. This could also affect you in love—you long to hear just the right thing at just the right moment. You can't help yourself when a heated debate is going on—you either walk away or get right in the middle. Your partner needs to be intelligent and must have good rationalization skills or you easily get bored. On the other hand, you like a mate with a touch of "simple." Someone who can lighten your moods and your affinity for self-pity is a welcome friend or partner. Mercury in Virgo goes well with Mercury in Aries, Pisces, Aquarius, Virgo, Cancer, Taurus, and Capricorn.

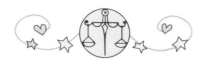

Chapter 7
Libra

Libra in love is a wonderful thing to behold—his eyes twinkle, he has a spring in his step. He has an innate sexiness and purity that comes through with each smile he throws your way. But he's a lot more complicated than he seems. In this chapter, we discover the real Libra and what he may be hiding behind his good looks.

Libra, the Fair

There are two ways to explain this title. First, she is fair in a physical sense—nice to look at. Second, she's fair. She needs to weigh out and decipher all the implications of things. Let's deal with the first.

Libra man is almost always handsome on some level. Libra woman has her own beauty. You would think Libra would be cocky about his good fortune in the looks department, but he's not. He also has a sweetness that makes him seem vulnerable. But he's not as simple as he seems. Instead, he looks to gain stability and security through other things—some of those worthwhile and some not.

 QUESTION?

Is Libra a fair judge of character?
It's hard to say. A more evolved Libra will take the time to weigh out the benefits and disadvantages of a friendship/love relationship and will come out with a pretty solid conclusion. A less evolved Libra will let fear get in the way of his good sense.

In other words, Libra's position in life—who he is, where he comes from, who his friends are, and who he's seen with—are important to Libra deep down. Though he doesn't come off as an opportunist, there's something very odd about Libra's social life. He has friends in different corners of the world but is extremely selective about the people he gets close to. You'll probably notice that Libra takes everything and everyone with a grain of salt. He has many friends but doesn't necessarily consider them real ones. It's a mistake for most people to think they know the real Libra. He's pensive and is constantly assessing situations in his head. But, for the most part, Libra pretty much tells it straight.

Mature versus Immature Libra

There are two very different kinds of Libras: the mature kind and the deeply immature kind. Age is not a factor. As a rule of thumb, though there are always exceptions, Libra woman tends to come into her own far earlier than Libra man. A mature Libra will approach you directly, have a conversation with you, and get to the heart of the matter. You'll feel like he's listened and heard what you said. A less mature Libra will strike you as confident, interesting, and somewhat mysterious. He'll go around a topic and let you do more of the talking—seemingly hoping that you'll somehow say the wrong thing. Or he'll simply provoke you, saying things he knows will either infuriate you or make you turn away from him.

Libra has emotional depth, but he doesn't know how to manage his feelings. He's also insecure, though he doesn't show it one bit. Though this Libra seems at ease with himself, in truth he's afraid of his own shadow. It's best to stay away from him until he understands what's important and what's not.

Eye of the Storm

Libra needs to be in control of his own destiny. If he feels pressured or sucked into something he doesn't want to be a part of, he instantly backs away. He also needs to decide when he wants to get romantically caught up and when he doesn't. For Libra, timing is everything.

She's also idealistic in a way that's not particularly romantic. Though she can be incredibly romantic and sweet—deep down, Libra is a real poet—she saves this for the person of her dreams. And just who is that? If a less mature Libra were to decide, she would create or invent a mate for herself. He'd be handsome and sexy, sweet, kind, smart, witty, bashful, modest, deep . . . the list goes on.

 ESSENTIAL

> Libra is pretty sure what kind of partner he wants. Though he's known to be fair, that's not always true when it comes to picking a mate. Libra is determined to find someone who fits the perfect image he has in his head.

Libra also tends (unwittingly) to create problems around him. In this way, he's like the eye of the storm—seemingly calm in the middle of it all while bedlam happens around him. Strangely enough, he also somehow manages to stir up trouble without actually getting involved. For example, he'll start a heated debate and then scoot off before he's drawn into it.

FACT

When Libra talks, she speaks the truth, but she doesn't always come out and say what she's thinking or feeling. She needs to be approached and asked. Then she'll say what's on her mind.

The Art of Attraction

Libra may be difficult to conquer. Libra man, for example, usually goes for the prettiest girl in the room. But tastes vary—what's beautiful to one may not appeal to another. At the very least, Libras tend to be born with a good aesthetic sense. Whether this particular trait comes out through his work or through his personal relationship says a lot about the kind of Libra you're dealing with. A Libra who incorporates his love of beauty into his everyday life is more balanced than a Libra who seeks perfection from the people around him.

Aside from that, Libra doesn't like her potential mate to be too aggressive. Courting, to a Libra, is like a dance—a tango, perhaps—slow and intricate. Libra is also a subtle flirt, but she doesn't like her partner to be too flirty with others. Though she's not as jealous as some other signs (like Scorpio or Cancer), she still doesn't like to compete with others for your attention.

Though Libra does like to be swept away with love, he can also get involved on a more superficial level. Libra, remember, is an Air sign; he can rationalize anything away. If a Libra decides he wants to have a fling, he has it—with no regrets. How do you know if Libra is playing with you or playing for keeps? Easy. Just ask him. Libra will tell you. He's not known to hide his intentions. In fact, he's as straight as they come.

 QUESTION?

What's the biggest problem in conquering a Libra?
Indecision. Libra doesn't get involved until she's 100 percent sure about you. And sometimes it takes her awhile to decide if she wants to risk it or not.

The Long Haul

Libra either gets married very late or very early. There's almost never a middle ground. Those who settle down early in life tend to choose poorly and may later regret it. Normally, though, when Libra finally marries, it's for keeps. She devotes herself to her other half and relies on him for sustenance. She can also be affectionate in private. Most Libras aren't keen to public displays of affection. They like to keep their home life at home.

Because Libra can easily separate romantic or sexual flings from real love and someone he intends to stay with, you should expect him to act accordingly. If it's a temporary love situation, he won't hesitate to cheat or look around while he's with you. If he wants you for keeps, though, he'll be faithful and true. Once again, ask. You'll get a straight answer one way or the other—and find out for real what you mean to him.

He/She: The Little Stuff Counts

While Virgo is more detail-oriented in noticing flaws in others, Libra, too, will pay attention to the little things. Libra men, for example, always go for women who are particularly well groomed. This doesn't mean that she has to be elegant or even always dressed up. Libra man likes women who can be casual with a pair of jeans, too. But he'll notice if her hair is cut nicely and done up and if her fingernails are polished and look pretty.

Though Libra likes out-there sexiness in a partner for a fling, she tends to lean to the more conservative side in hunting for a future mate. Libra woman also likes a man who seems capable and rock steady. Libra is very good at accomplishing whatever task she puts her mind to—whether it's rock climbing, flying a plane, or selling ice to an Eskimo. Unlike Gemini, she doesn't talk to fill in the gaps. She likes a partner to understand the benefits of silence.

Pillow Talk: Signs in the Bedroom

How much a Libra suffers earlier on in life will normally determine how mature he is. Libras who grow up with a sense of discipline, not spoiled, will be quite evolved. This carries over to the bedroom. A less mature Libra man, for example, will need to feel completely in charge in bed. He'll pick a woman who is demure or inexperienced for a long-term mate. For a fling, he'll choose a woman whose tastes run on the kinky side.

All Libras love sex. Actually, their libidos may even be the biggest in the zodiac. They also have a hidden side (like Virgo does) that only comes out with either partners they feel comfortable with or partners they don't think they'll keep around for long. Verbally, they like to test out a partner.

The Secret Libra Man

Many times, Libra man will speak with his eyes. Though he talks a good game and he might even be touchy-feely, this means nothing. You'll know if a Libra man is serious about you by the way he looks at you—it'll be different from the way he looks at others. His eyes have the power to pierce your soul. You'll feel it in your gut.

 ESSENTIAL

If you're seducing a Libra man, let him seduce you. If you've already been intimate with him, you can be bolder. Stare into his eyes, and touch his stomach softly. He'll melt.

One good way to capture a Libra man is to let him come to you. Ignore him a little, but always be polite. He'll be waiting for you on your doorstep when you come home. Also remember that Libra is expecting you to make the wrong move. He'll watch you from afar and even have his friends keep an eye on you. Libras are notorious observers when it comes to love. Any indecent or inappropriate behavior—including excessive flirting or affection with the opposite sex—will turn a Libra off pronto.

Libras can also be sensitive to touch. If he lets you, give him a massage. Once Libra is comfortable with you, you can tell him what you like, too. Let Libra man steer the bed play to where he wants it to go and try to go along with it. He'll open up more with his thoughts and feelings in bed.

The Secret Libra Woman

She likes men who are skilled in the art of making love. To her, sex is really art, and it must be beautiful in some way. This doesn't mean that she must always be in love to make love. On the contrary, Libra woman is just as good at separating the real thing from a sexual adventure. Though she prefers to be completely swept away in love, she's capable of having fun, too.

Libra woman tends to be quite independent. She can sometimes be more aggressive in bed than Libra man. She knows what she wants and usually gets it. Though she can be a heartbreaker, she always tells it straight. She won't lead you on, for example, if she doesn't intend to follow through. Though it might take her a little while to decide, once she does, she's crystal clear.

FACT

> Libra woman tends to have lots of energy. This carries over into the bedroom as well. She'll look for a partner who wants to go all night—not one who seems to think that "foreplay" means something to do with golf.

Sun Love Matches

Libra tends to be slippery in love. He's hard to catch and even harder to figure out. Because Libra can be idealistic about what kind of partner he wants, it's difficult to get into his head and know just what he's looking for. Do keep in mind that Libra always has a set image of what he wants. He's not going to change his ideas on a whim.

Read on to learn about compatible matches for Libra woman.

Libra Man

This is a hard match to predict. If there's a lot of Earth in the rest of their charts (one or both), they go together fabulously. Libra woman, though, may take the lead, and this may irk Libra man who likes to feel like he's in control of things—even if he's not. This has to do with a question of timing. If both are ready for something serious, they can be a great couple. In bed, things are creative and adventurous if Libra man lets Libra woman get her way. Overall, this is a probable long-term relationship, with a good chance for marriage.

 ALERT!

If you want to be with Libra, find out exactly what she is looking for first. If you're not it, don't waste your time. Libra won't fall in love if she doesn't want to—just as true, by the way, of Libra man.

Scorpio Man

Scorpio man enchants Libra woman at first. What bothers her, though, is that even if she usually gets a straight answer from him, she senses he's hiding something. Scorpio man, too, doesn't seem as grounded as Libra would like. He plays games and can give her a guilt trip. Plus, he's moody. Though the sex can be fantastic, Libra is more creative while Scorpio is more intense. These two can really laugh together though. This can be a possible long-term thing, with marriage possible on the horizon.

Sagittarius Man

The male Archer doesn't like to show how much he needs the company of a loving woman. He gets a bit stressed when things don't go his way, and Libra woman doesn't know how to handle him. She may need a softer touch. Sagittarius also needs her to boost his ego in bed. He's a lusty lover—she is too—but he goes more by instinct. Intellectually, they inspire each other. This can be a possible long-term thing, but it's not a probable marriage.

Capricorn Man

Capricorn and Libra can get into power struggles. She needs to let him lead. Also, Capricorn man may not be refined enough for Libra lady. If he is out to please her—going where she wants and dressing as she likes—they'll get along fine. Though Capricorn likes to stay home more than gregarious Libra, they don't have too many problems finding a middle ground. In bed, Capricorn absolutely needs to dominate, and Libra woman is usually more than willing, in this case, to let him do so. This can be a very possible long-term thing, with marriage possible too.

Aquarius Man

Aquarius man and Libra woman? Who would've thought? The two are different in many ways, and yet they're both Air signs. Somehow, though, they balance each other out. Though Libra is more conservative than Aquarius, he inspires her to be more creative. In return, she teaches him about art and about the finer things in life. In bed, they have similar styles and it sizzles. Aquarius may be a bit kinkier though. This can be a very possible long-term relationship. It's also a probable marriage.

⒠ ALERT!

Aquarius man has an unfaithful streak. If he's committed to being faithful with Libra woman, this can work. If he's not, Libra will walk!

Pisces Man

To Libra, Pisces man is just plain weird—but she likes that. Though she gets the feeling that he's just going along with everything she says, she doesn't mind it at all. Art seems to be a common theme between these two. They're also both quite conservative in their manner. The success of this match depends on whether Pisces can stand up to Libra. If he's a dreamer, Libra will get frustrated. If he's as independent as she is, they'll get along well. However, bed is another matter. Pisces may not be able to keep up with Libra's energy. This can be a possible long-term partnership. Marriage isn't probable, but it's not impossible, either.

Aries Man

Aries man swaggers in and charms the charming Libra woman. She fascinates him; he fascinates her. But Aries man needs to be the center of attention, and Libra woman gets the spotlight without even trying. Aries holds her back. She also gets annoyed when he doesn't stick to his word—which she does—and when he shows up late all the time. They can have a great affair if Aries man respects Libra woman. All in all, this can be a great fling, whether short-term or even a little longer. It's just not a probable marriage.

Taurus Man

Though Taurus is likely to fall in love first, Libra woman will keep him reeled in until she feels it herself. These two inspire each other and are dynamic together. Libra has all kinds of moral, honorable behavior that Taurus admires. The only problem these two could have, however, is Taurus's thin skin—Libra criticizes, and Taurus shrinks away in humiliation. Plus, he won't confront the situation. In bed, they make a perfect match. If Libra can impress Taurus with her strong hold on finances, this can be a probable long-term relationship with a good chance for marriage.

Gemini Man

Gemini and Libra together are the wildest, most fun, outrageous couple in the room. Just don't get in between these two—their bond is strong and ferocious. Though Gemini is more possessive and jealous than Libra woman, the gender combination here works (Gemini man, Libra woman). The other way around might be a bit more difficult. Though Gemini can get kinkier in bed, Libra can keep up if she wants to. If they can each accept the little skeletons hidden in their respective closets, this can be a good long-term love and a very probable marriage.

ALERT!

Gemini should beware of asking too many questions of Libra! She doesn't like giving away too many personal things about her life right away. When Gemini interrogates, Libra gets wary and eventually weary of Gemini.

Cancer Man

Cancer and Libra are seemingly from two different planets. Though they can have a wonderful friendship—talking for hours about the strange and unusual—it may end there. Cancer feels. Libra thinks. Cancer doesn't rationalize; Libra does nothing but. If Libra woman can always swing Cancer's opinion to her side, this has a chance. Sexually, though, Cancer man may not completely understand what Libra woman needs. If he's willing to let her shine and doesn't get too clingy or possessive, this could work. But most likely, though this is a possible long-term thing, it's not a probable marriage.

Leo Man

Leo and Libra? They're both passionate—but about completely different things. Leo is passionate about love, whereas Libra gets more excited about life in general. He takes romance more seriously. She likes her independence. Libra loves the fact that Leo is warm, generous, and treats her with respect. If she has some Fire signs in the rest of her chart, this can be a possible long-term relationship. It's not a probable marriage, but it is possible.

 ESSENTIAL

Leo is unduly impressed with the way Libra follows through with everything. He knows she's worthy of him, and he loves to show her off. However, in bed their relationship can work only if Libra lets Leo have all the control.

Virgo Man

When these two get together, watch out! They can either click completely or rub each other the wrong way, causing chaos around them. Talk about verbal warfare—these two can fight dirty. And though this will inevitably turn Virgo man on, Libra woman will probably head for the hills. In bed, though, there is no more perfect lover for Libra woman. They heat each other up and adore each other's style. If Virgo man can soften a little and Libra can hold back the judgmental comments, this can be a possible long-term situation. It's also a very possible marriage.

Love Planets: Venus and Mercury

Libra in your chart always gives someone a little mystique—charm, beauty from within, and a certain aura of ingenuity. It also makes you consider your options before diving in, positioning them against one another to understand whether the advantages outweigh the disadvantages. Also, Libra is always attracted to beauty in some way: through art, people, or surroundings.

Venus in Libra

More than anything, a person with Venus in Libra loves being in love. Though you're highly selective about a mate—picky even—you don't like being alone for long stretches of time. No one can force you to do what you don't want, and the worst thing a partner could do is pressure you to make a decision you're not ready to make. Venus in Libra goes well with Venus in Aquarius, Gemini, Libra, Taurus, Virgo, and Capricorn.

 FACT

> You're very versatile in bed and in life. You seek the perfect balance from a love mate— you want someone who's your best friend and lover at the same time.

Mercury in Libra

Intellectually, you're a smart cookie, and you're resourceful, too. Your know-how doesn't come just from books—it comes from doing. Besides being familiar with literature, you've got what they call "street-smarts." People like to hear you talk because you know what makes a good story, and you're not keen on exaggerating. Talking about love may be your only downfall. You sometimes give too much away when you talk about a partner. This could be embarrassing to others or make you seem a bit flighty. No bother, though. You're still charming and fabulous—and deep down you know it, without ever giving off a pretentious or even a slightly cocky air. Mercury in Libra goes well with Mercury in Gemini, Virgo, Libra, Aquarius, Cancer, Capricorn, and Sagittarius.

Chapter 8
Scorpio

Scorpio has sex appeal off the charts. When he falls in love, it's deeply and utterly. The only problem is getting him there—and then keeping him. In this chapter, find out how to capture dark Scorpio's heart.

The Dark One

Scorpio always seems to have something dangerous about him. Perhaps you can't put your finger on it, but it's always there. He broods, mumbles under his breath, and you feel like he's always thinking. He also comes off as easygoing and free, though you know he's a force to deal with when he's angry—a virtual tornado when he actually lets loose.

Secretive

Yes, Scorpio always has something simmering just beneath the surface. She's crafty, and she knows how to make things go her way. Scorpio also speaks only half of what's on her mind. Most call her secretive, and she is. But there's something else—she's a private person. She's reserved. Though she comes off as friendly and open, Scorpio is very closed about the inner workings of her mind—more than she'll ever let on.

 QUESTION?

What do most Scorpios fear most?
Discovery. They're a little embarrassed about the oddities that go through their heads. Therefore, they're good at showing you only what they want you to see.

Proud

Scorpio is also a very proud creature. She's willful, stubborn, and determined to get her way. And the reason she's so hard to figure out is that she's more a contradiction in terms than most other signs of the zodiac. Here are a few examples:

- Scorpio tends to get more obsessed with someone who's not good for him (like Taurus).
- Scorpio will hunt down a potential mate, not relenting until she falls in love with him.
- Scorpio is a very private soul, but he hates feeling lonely.
- Scorpio wants you to tell all your secrets, but he won't tell any of his own. All Scorpios have something hidden in their past—they're not the open books they seem to be.
- Scorpio seems easygoing and cool one minute and then suddenly snaps, becoming anxious or angry.
- Scorpio overworks himself to the point of complete exhaustion, complains about it, but does nothing to resolve the problem.

Unpredictable

In short, Scorpio is, at the very least, entirely unpredictable. She's a mystery—that's for sure. So, how do you snag Scorpio's heart? It's not easy. There are, however, some tricks and tips in this chapter. First, read up on what Scorpio is really thinking. Then, go to the section on love matches. By the end of these pages, you'll be a pro.

You're Mine

Okay, Scorpio is incredibly jealous and possessive, but he's also protective. A Scorpio will defend you within two inches of his life (the way Leo also would). He's smart, and when he's in love—or believes he is—he's really in love. Fortunately, you can tell whether Scorpio is or is not. In the beginning, he'll pursue you. He'll be generous and affectionate. When this behavior stops or wanes, you'll know you're starting to lose him. Something must be done, or the relationship will fade away altogether.

 ALERT!

> Think scorpion. Think deadly. Don't ever cross a Scorpio! She'll sneak up from behind. And she can be vengeful and crafty about it— knowing exactly how to push your buttons and possibly even hurt you.

Just keep in mind that a Scorpio will stay in a situation longer than he should. Because of this, when he breaks, he usually does it in a harsh or uncaring way. This is done really to protect himself. If he leaves you when he still has some feelings, he knows he's going to suffer. (Once again, Scorpios are more sensitive than they seem.)

Be advised, however, that when Scorpio finally ends it, it's over. You may be able to seduce him once or twice after, but only if he's convinced that you don't have any remaining feelings for him—that you're not looking for something more. This is the only way Scorpios show their practical side in love.

The Art of Attraction

Scorpio is all about transformation. Just associating with one will change your life in some way. While Aquarius, for example, goes for the strange or unique partner, Scorpio is drawn to opposites. She wants someone who can really go wild and let loose in the bedroom and then be able to dine among the best of them. Sex is also very important to Scorpio. She has the ability to make it good for both of you (Scorpio man, too).

 FACT

> Here's a tip: Scorpio men love to be complimented on intimate things like their clothes or their smell. So do Scorpio women. Give them a slow, sultry kiss and whisper it to them in their ear. They'll love it.

In fact, the best time to have an important conversation is after lovemaking. She lets her guard down, and she'll be more willing to hear what you have to say. Get her to laugh a little before you start. Scorpio loves to laugh and does it too rarely. Incidentally, you'll also want to be neat around Scorpio—even when you throw your clothes around in wild love play. Scorpio is very orderly and clean, and she expects the same of you. Don't think of looking in her closets, though. Scorpio, though neat, is a notorious pack rat.

The Long Haul

Scorpio can be difficult to deal with sometimes. He has certain unique requirements. Most likely, he likes to hang around people his partner won't necessarily like or approve of. For this reason, Scorpio tends to marry later than most. But Scorpio loves love, and he wants to be in love forever. He loves children and makes a wonderful, caring father who will do anything for his children. Scorpio woman, too, has great instincts with children. The only thing Scorpio must watch out for is temper—most Scorpios have one. They let the anger build up instead of releasing it, and it all comes out in a whoosh. Though Scorpio would never in a million years willfully hurt a child, he or she must be equally careful to keep this natural tendency at bay.

Is Scorpio in love with you? Not sure how he feels about you? There is a subtle test you can give your Scorpio mate. It does count as game playing, but if you really need to know, just flirt with one of his friends. At the very least, he'll tell you about all you his friend's bad points (hoping to assure himself the winner's place, next to you). At the very worst, he'll haul you out of the restaurant and kiss you senseless, so you know for sure just who you really belong to. Scorpio is the most jealous of the signs. It's a sneaky way to snatch him, and, perhaps, a manipulative way to keep him. But, hey, it works.

 ALERT!

> Just make sure not to cross the line! A Scorpio, in vengeance, will do the same back to you. And who can resist a Scorpio's sexy, stunning charms? Be careful not to make Scorpio too jealous—his pride may just out-weigh his need for you.

He/She: The Little Stuff Counts

Scorpio, normally, is pretty informal. Although she can dress up on a moment's notice, she usually prefers to dress comfortably. However, she won't mind how you dress and may not even notice. Scorpio man, in particular, will be unduly impressed by the sight of a beautiful woman in a tight dress—tasteful and conservative, not tacky. On her side, a Scorpio woman will be drawn to a man with a pleasing scent. Actually, all Scorpios have very acute senses—except for hearing, which usually tends to be as bad as his or her other senses are good. (Although sometimes they just pretend not to hear you.)

Scorpio is also extremely subjective to touch and taste. Many Scorpio women and men are wonderful cooks once they get a little practice. Cook for him, and make sure the food has diverse tastes—combine salty, sweet, and spicy, for example. This is an aphrodisiac for Scorpio. Stroke his thigh, and you probably won't get to finish your meal—Scorpio will have you in bed before you've had your last bite.

 ESSENTIAL

> Though Scorpio's hearing isn't as sharp as his other senses, he is gifted with a silky, sultry voice—it's strangely sensual. Most Scorpios, too, like sexy voices. While on the phone or sitting right next to him, whisper something tantalizing into his ear. This will work.

Pillow Talk: Signs in the Bedroom

All Scorpios are incredibly accomplished lovers. They have an innate sexual instinct and their passion rides them, and you. You'll feel like you're swept away with dark, alluring Scorpio. But he won't seduce you unless his mind is there. Try to get him to laugh at himself. Scorpio places too much importance, sometimes, on the little things. He gets wrapped up in details and fails to see the big picture.

The Secret Scorpio Man

Scorpio man tends to get obsessed about things. It may be you in the beginning. But once he has you, the obsession will probably shift to his work. Work and livelihood is very important to Scorpio man. His coworkers, most likely, think of him as a dedicated soul—difficult as he is. He's a perfectionist. When things don't go his way, he has a hard time dealing with it, fretting and pouting in his free time.

This little tidbit is important to know because it may spill into your sex and relationship time together. Once you relax Scorpio sufficiently, though, he will pour his passion and dedication into you. His perfectionism, in this case, is directed to an entirely different goal. He'll want to seduce you completely and utterly. Here's one thing you don't have to worry about: Though Scorpio man can dominate in bed, he won't mind letting you take the reins once in awhile. It depends on his mood. The key to success in the bedroom with Scorpio is to follow his lead. Rest assured: Instinctively and passionately, Scorpio's got your number.

 ESSENTIAL

> Scorpio man actually feels more than he lets on. If he confesses strong feelings for you, chances are they're even stronger than you imagine.

The Secret Scorpio Woman

Though she's outgoing, funny, and smart, she's got a lot going on under the surface. She seems so open and liberal with her feelings; instead, she has lots of personal issues that secretly haunt her. Whether these problems have to do with her relationship, her family, or her work, she'll entrust her skeletons to one person and one person only: her other half, her love. In other words, you'll know whether she loves you and trusts you—for Scorpio, the two go hand in hand—if she confesses her deepest, darkest secrets.

But Scorpio woman is, indeed, a private soul. She, too, can be coerced to talk more freely in bed. After making love, she lets her guard down. This is a perfect time to find her demons and get her to open up to you. For Scorpio, sex is like air—she needs it to survive.

 FACT

> Scorpio woman is also sensual. Though she may come off as conservative in public, she's passionate and playful in bed. She loves to be in love. She'll worship you with her actions more than words, but once you have her heart, you have a true, loving soul who would bring you the moon if she could.

Sun Love Matches

Scorpio men and women are very instinctive. Unfortunately, they sometimes ignore their instincts in friendship and in love. With friends, they keep relations going for a purpose—mostly if the rapport is important for work contacts or social means. On the other hand, sex can sway them greatly in love. If a mate is not right for them, they'll know it, but they'll stay if things are powerful in the bedroom. However, when Scorpios are truly in love, they'll tell you so. And then they'll make you their world. Scorpios go well with Water and Fire, the other "feeling" signs. Read on to discover the love combinations for Scorpio woman.

Scorpio Man

These two go together so well that it's a little scary. However, the perfect, happy couple they appear to be in public is sometimes different from what they experience alone at home. Scorpio man is possessive. Instinctively, he needs her to need him. He may criticize just a little too much, but in bed, the fireworks are hot and heavy. If Scorpio woman can let Scorpio man feel in charge, this can be a probable long-term relationship. The two also have a good chance for marriage.

 ALERT!

Scorpio man is so crazy about Scorpio woman that he tries to control her. In fact, he puts her down sometimes simply to keep her close to him. He doesn't want her to go too far, out of his reach.

Sagittarius Man

Sagittarius man is a lot more direct and blunt than Scorpio woman, and the one thing he wants from her is the truth. She gives it to him as much as she can but has a hard time unmasking herself. However, if the Archer is patient, Scorpio will reveal all her hidden mysteries. These two go well together, even though trust could be an issue from the get-go. In bed, Sagittarius has all the right moves if he doesn't doubt himself too much. All in all, though, this can be a fiery, passionate union. It is a very possible long-term thing and also a possible marriage.

 FACT

Sagittarius man needs to trust his feelings and go with it. If he's looking for too much assurance in the beginning, he may not get it from Scorpio woman. He must give her time to open up, or this love combo won't work!

Capricorn Man

In the beginning, Capricorn man will capture Scorpio's attention. She's drawn to his stability, to his friendly, easygoing manner, and to his looks. But Capricorn man has other things on his agenda. He has trouble figuring her out, and this bothers him. He'd like things to go more smoothly. She'd like him to be more affectionate. This match truly depends on what

Capricorn has in the rest of his chart. If his Venus is in a Water or even a Fire sign, they may have a chance. Most likely, this is a possible long-term thing. It's also a possible but not likely marriage.

Aquarius Man

Aquarius man is fascinated by the strange, the unpredictable. If Scorpio woman can give him the freedom to roam, he might even fall for her. Chances are, though, he'd like to let the relationship go with the flow, and she wants promises right away. In bed, Scorpio woman loves it that nothing shocks Aquarius. She can be as free as she wants and, though she may hold back, she likes the security of knowing that nothing is taboo—except emotional surrender. (Aquarians are notoriously distant in this respect.) This is a possible long-term thing, but it's not a probable marriage.

Pisces Man

Love and sex isn't rocket science, and Scorpio wishes Pisces man would understand this. Sometimes they misinterpret each other. She just wants to make things simpler, and here Pisces gives Scorpio woman the kind of affection and devotion she's looking for. Pisces doesn't mind so much that she's possessive of him. In fact, he kind of likes it. They both like to touch, and the sensuality in this union can be deep and powerful. If Scorpio can adjust to Pisces' schedule—he has more energy than she does—this can be a good long-term relationship, even a very possible marriage.

QUESTION?

> **How does Scorpio seduce Pisces?**
> With mystery. Pisces loves to solve a puzzle. The
> intrigue will keep him coming back for more.
> He also loves music and romantic settings.

Aries Man

Cool, sexy, dominant Aries fascinates Scorpio
woman completely. In return, she intrigues him.
Unfortunately, Scorpio can try to hold Aries back when
it comes to his socializing. This can be disastrous since
he needs to feel free. Once he has the option to roam,
he'll most likely run back to her side. In bed, they're
both instinctive and each can give the other the perfect
dose of loving. If Scorpio is willing to let Aries shine,
this can be a probable long-term thing, with marriage a
possibility in the long run.

Taurus Man

Normally Earth and Water signs don't mix very well.
But something else is at work here with Taurus and
Scorpio. They're both sensitive, and they can both be
traditional (though this is more likely of Taurus).
Sexually, they're the two hottest signs of the zodiac.
Scorpio is more instinctive and sexual, while Taurus is
more sensual. If Scorpio woman can take it slow and let
Taurus lead, they will have no problems in bed. On the
contrary, if the sex is no good, these two will not last.

This can be a possible long-term relationship. It's not a probable marriage but, strangely enough, still possible.

 ALERT!

> Watch out! Both Scorpio and Taurus have an obsessive side. In this case, Taurus might idealize and fantasize about Scorpio man, putting him on a pedestal that he may or may not deserve. Maintaining a balance between these two is difficult but it can be done.

Gemini Man

Scorpio woman is not likely to get a word in edgewise with Gemini man. Though he'll capture her attention for brief stretches of time, she knows better than to wait for more. Gemini won't put in the time to break down her barriers and get to know the real woman behind the façade. Deep down, that's just what she's hoping for in a long-term mate: acknowledgment and acceptance. In bed, Gemini man confuses Scorpio woman with his role-playing and mumbling about "what he's going to do with her." "Just do it already," she thinks. In the long run, this can be a positive long-term thing, but it's not a probable marriage.

Cancer Man

These two inflame each other across the board, spiritually, mentally, and even physically. Though Cancer probably needs more security than Scorpio does—even in the beginning—she can keep Cancer man happy in almost all regards. Both are notorious game players, and Cancer man can be quite the Casanova at times. Scorpio woman, though, is intense enough to keep his attention. The only problem in this match is the way these two fight. They go all out and bare their souls— without thought of the consequences of saying what first comes to mind. As a result, they can get nasty with each other, and the two have trouble forgiving afterward. At the end, however, this can be a very good long-term thing, with a good chance for marriage.

 FACT

> Cancer man just loves provoking Scorpio woman to the point of hysteria. Her passion and anger is what he's after—he lives for the challenge of calming her and making her his own.

Leo Man

Leo man simply can't figure out what to do with Scorpio woman. She misinterprets and misunderstands what he says—and he's pretty direct. He adores her and makes her know it. But she doesn't trust him. In this case, the lowest common denominator of happiness really does apply. Scorpio becomes sullen or moody and brings Leo man down with her. Leo and Scorpio in bed, though, make a fantastic pair. When they get closer, they have passionate, sexy trysts and can laugh a lot together. If Leo can side with Scorpio when she complains and wait patiently until she snaps out of it, this can be a possible long-term relationship and also a possible marriage.

Virgo Man

Virgo and Scorpio are like night and day. In fact, they're more likely to talk about and analyze their relationship together than they are to have one. Though Scorpio doesn't let on, she'd like just a little more attention and affection than Virgo man is willing to give. Scorpio has more worldly, glamorous tastes than Virgo. If Virgo has a lot of Water or Fire in his chart, they could get along well. Still, this is probably not a long-term thing, and it's an unlikely marriage as well, but it's certainly possible.

 ESSENTIAL

Both Virgo man and Scorpio woman find it difficult to open up. In bed, they can have fun if Virgo admits to his baser instincts. Scorpio, though, is impressed with Virgo's get-right-down-to-it style and his good business sense.

Libra Man

Libra's occasionally distant emotional nature intrigues Scorpio, but he makes her wary, too. She gets insecure if he criticizes her, and she senses that she will never live up to his perfectionist ideals. To Libra, mysterious, sensual Scorpio is a real handful, and he's not quite sure if he's ready to deal with her expansive ways. A good roll in the hay will change his mind, if he's willing. But Libra is picky with his bed partners. He teases but only sometimes follows through, running hot and cold emotionally as well as physically. If Libra doesn't scare Scorpio off with his "free love" ways, this can be a possible long-term relationship. It's a possible, but not probable, marriage.

Love Planets: Venus and Mercury

Scorpio in the rest of your chart always adds a bit of mystery, intrigue, and even sensuality. Scorpios are always intense and passionate. They also know how to capture the attention and affection of the opposite sex—without really trying. They're not flirtatious, like aggressive Gemini. They're more laid back: "I'm here. I'm it. I'm cool." And your Venus, or even Mercury, will add that extra "oomph" to your personality. Below, compare the other aspects in Scorpio.

Venus in Scorpio

Once again, sex is extremely important to you. Though you may even equate love with great love-making, you want all experiences you share with a mate to be intense and passionate. You can't help being possessive and jealous. Venus in Scorpio has an addictive side, too. Not just in terms of love—also to alcohol, perhaps, nicotine, or even antidepressants. Self-pity could be your biggest downfall. When you're in love and feeling happy, though, your mood and good nature are contagious. Venus in Scorpio goes well with Venus in Cancer, Scorpio, Pisces, Sagittarius, and Taurus.

Mercury in Scorpio

You truly care what other people think and that's good. You're instinctive and somehow know how to turn a conversation to your advantage. Charm is your middle name. When you speak, people listen. In fact, you may even have a sexy, sultry, or interesting voice. You like one-on-one deep talks rather than big groups and chatting with many different people. A romantic dinner with someone you love, for example, is an ideal evening for you. You are definitely not superficial. Mercury in Scorpio pairs with Mercury in Pisces, Cancer, Scorpio, Aries, Taurus, and Sagittarius.

Chapter 9

Sagittarius

Sagittarius has two sides, one serious, and one that's extremely playful. He can seem like one person and then change his character entirely. These aren't moods—this is *him*. How do you get to the heart of Sagittarius? What do you do to win him? In this chapter, find out what gets Sagittarius but good.

The Renaissance Man (or Woman)

For Sagittarius, learning something new is like breathing. She craves adventure and intense experiences. But here's the paradox. She may want to skydive, sail, learn foreign languages, conquer new worlds, yet all the while she's looking for a partner who's something of an opposing force—one who will balance her out. In other words, Sagittarius wants to shine, and she needs someone who'll let her, who'll come along for the ride of a lifetime and stand next to her with a quiet strength. The perfect Sagittarius partner has to be a tough cookie, laugh at all her jokes, and have fun with her. For Sagittarius, a boring life with her work or with a love partner is like not living at all.

 ESSENTIAL

> If you want to get Sagittarius's attention, listen. If he feels like you're "yes"-ing him to get out of the conversation, he'll become annoyed. Hear Sagittarius when he speaks— he has a lot of interesting things to say!

In fact, Sagittarius has absolutely no patience with people who just don't "get it." He can be intolerant to the point of disgust if he believes someone is going about something "the wrong way." For Sagittarius, in fact, there's only one right way: his way. If you're a Fire sign or an Air sign, make sure to give Sagittarius his due. If you argue with him, he'll never see your side; he'll only think of you as a troublemaker. If you want to be with Sagittarius, let him think he's in control (even when he's not and knows it). Sagittarius—man or woman—need to be heard and understood.

R-E-S-P-E-C-T

For Sagittarius, it's essential that his authority is respected and acknowledged. In important moments, it will infuriate him if you joke or fail to take a situation seriously. It's almost as if he was born with a chip on his shoulder when it comes to being given consideration. He also has a secret violent streak that can come out unexpectedly. Do yourself a favor, and always make Sagittarius feel like a treasure.

Did we say treasure? Are you ready for this? Sagittarius is one of the most fun, interesting, talented, ironical signs of the zodiac. He has a knack for being good at everything he does. One minute he's telling you that he's an awful dancer; the next, he's sweeping you off your feet. Why? Kind, fun, and sexy as he is, Sagittarius is modest. He'll be the first to say that he's not that great—when you know that the exact opposite is true. He has two main motives. He likes compliments, and he's a perfectionist.

Candid. Honest. Direct to a fault. These are all good descriptions of Sagittarius. Though Sagittarius is a teddy bear, sweet and sensitive with the person he loves, he has absolutely no tact. He'll give it to you straight, letting loose with the first thing that comes to mind—and we all know how much trouble this causes. No matter. When Sagittarius is really in love, you'll know it. He'll tell you, and you can believe him completely. Sagittarius never says he's in love if he's not.

 FACT

> When Sagittarius starts criticizing you, just remember that he's his own worst critic, too. These rules don't only apply to you. They apply to him as well. In fact, he'll tell you his faults even before you discover them yourself.

The Art of Attraction

Sagittarius likes to do exactly the opposite of what she's told. If you pressure or (heaven forbid) try to manipulate her in some way, she'll smell you out in a second—and she won't like it, not one bit. But don't worry about giving Sagittarius a challenge. She's built for it. In fact, Sagittarius likes to work a little for love. If she gets what she wants too easily, it's not going to hold her attention for more than a second. However, once the relationship starts, Sagittarius wants things to go smoothly. If the personal rapport is not working out, or Sagittarius feels the two of you have different ways of handling things, Sagittarius will be out the door before you can say "wait."

ESSENTIAL

If a Sagittarius walks out on you, let her simmer for a few hours. Then make your next approach with a very calm, sweet demeanor. Tell her she was right. Arguing or trying to prove your point will never work with a Sagittarius.

The Long Haul

Sagittarius is not as independent as he seems. He instinctively knows whom to trust, and he likes good company. Though he seems just fine by himself, he lives to have a strong, wonderful companion by his side. Like all Fire signs, Sagittarius is an idealist and a perfectionist. He will not "settle" when it comes to love. Ironically enough, Sagittarius can be either the biggest player in the zodiac or the most devoted, loyal partner. Sagittarius honors his commitments, and his word is as good as gold.

 QUESTION?

What's a good way to know if Sagittarius is in love?
Ask him. He'll tell you. Sagittarius isn't big on flowery words of love and devotion, but his feelings are intense and sincere, regardless of whether he voices them.

He/She: The Little Stuff Counts

How should you dress for a Sagittarius? Sagittarius doesn't like showy, ostentatious dressers. He's more likely to notice your smile or your eyes before the color of shirt or brand of jeans you're wearing. Here's a tip, though: If Sagittarius is on a cusp bordering with Capricorn, he'll be slightly opportunistic. You can impress him by dropping names, telling him you travel a lot, or letting on that you have a close friend with a sailboat and villa by the sea. He'll be yours. (This works if he has Capricorn or a lot of Earth in his chart, too.) On the other hand, if he's near Scorpio or has a lot of Water in his chart, you're more likely to impress him with languages, music, good wine, and any kind of ethnic food.

 ESSENTIAL

All Sagittarius people love new experiences. Talk about how you crave adventure and live to travel. Ask him to take you somewhere you've never been. He will.

But don't expect Sagittarius to fall to her knees and tell you she worships the ground you walk on. Sagittarius speaks ten times more with action than with words. Though she can talk about anything, something gets her tongue when it comes to romantic words of love. A mate of a Sagittarius who comes to accept this will be very satisfied, though. Whatever she does say will mean much more than the same thing from someone who throws compliments around like they're nothing. Beyond that, both physically and sexually, you'll definitely get her point.

 FACT

> Though every Sagittarius has a spiritual side, this sign is the least likely to believe in astrology, destiny, or even religion. If you ask someone their sign and they say, "I don't believe in it," nine out of ten times, you've stumbled on a Sagittarius!

Pillow Talk: Signs in the Bedroom

Sagittarius cannot resist a real challenge. For love, it's got to be there. For sex, this goes double. And don't even think of playing hard to get in the beginning and then letting him have your heart and soul. Real love mates of Sagittarius know that continuing the flirtation throughout their life together means issuing a challenge and letting him "come and get it." Give Sagittarius everything he wants, and he'll take it with him when he walks out the door.

The Secret Sagittarius Man

Sagittarius is one of the most macho signs of the zodiac. If you tell him he can't do something, he'll do it just for the sake of proving himself. You want to get

Sagittarius into bed? Tell him he can't have you, and he'll stop at nothing to show you who's boss. Sagittarius man can also appear emotionally distant. Don't let it fool you. He's passionate, clever, instinctive, and very sexual. In bed, let Sagittarius lead. Tell him to talk to you. He knows exactly what to do, what to say, and when to say it.

He can, however, definitely keep sex and love on different planes, so watch out! Again, ask him what he's after, and he'll tell you. But insult a Sagittarius man on his lovemaking or his intelligence, and you'll never see him again. He'll take it in stride and bounce right back, but he's a lot more sensitive than he seems. And, when it comes down to it, he's a realist. No matter how in love he is, he's not a slave to his passions (or a masochist) like some other signs—Taurus or Cancer, for example.

The Secret Sagittarius Woman

She's all woman. She knows herself well and knows her limits. She's not afraid of love or the emotions that go with it. She's all fire and passion, and she's a great friend, lover, and confidante. But don't be fooled. She'll let herself be conquered only if she wants to be. How do you spark a Sagittarius woman's interest? Here are a few tips:

- Don't play hard to get. Be hard to get.
- Never talk about things you're not sure about. Instead, ask her to tell you about them.
- Listen to her.

- Be honest.
- Be modest, but charming.
- Always be a gentleman, and treat her with respect.
- Don't be a pushover. Stand up for yourself.
- Make her laugh, and make sure you laugh at her jokes.
- Show her you have a life outside of her.
- Talk in front of her to friends about how wonderful she is.

Above all, don't fawn all over Sagittarius woman. She won't trust or like you for it, and she certainly won't go to bed with you. Sagittarius doesn't mind a little public display of affection if she's into you. If she's not, she'll be cool as a cucumber. Though Sagittarius woman is never haughty, and never a snob, if she's nice to you, it doesn't mean she's in love with you. In bed, go by instinct. They'll be time for wild, uncensored sex and also time to make it slow and dreamy. In bed, too, Sagittarius lady is more likely to say how she feels about you. Make sure you let her know how you feel as well.

 ESSENTIAL

Sagittarius—both men and women—have one true defect that you'll just have to accept if you want to be with them: timing in social situations. They're likely to say the wrong thing to the wrong person. Reason: They're candid, open, and honest . . . to a fault!

Sun Love Matches

Passionate, sexy, fierce, and even a bit dangerous, Sagittarius is potent and will look for a partner who's potent as well. Just keep in mind that Sagittarius likes to be the ruler. If he gets involved with bossy Leo or demanding Aries, it can work because the fire is there . . . but only if he's given his respect and his due. Authority is everything to Sagittarius. Sagittarius goes well with Water signs, too, which seem to bring out the best in him. They also dote and give him the security and stability he secretly longs for. Read on to learn about the love compatibility matches for a Sagittarius woman.

Sagittarius Man

These two really know how to have a good time together. They're passionate about all the same things, and if there's one little thing they don't agree on, they understand how to give the other the time and space required to get over it.

 FACT

There are only two problems with the match between Sagittarius man and woman: the fighting and the making up. For one, neither Sagittarius will back down in a fight. Making up becomes a problem when Sagittarius craves a soft, stable, nurturing hand to turn to when he's willing to be coaxed.

They both know how to play, to love, and to make love. They have to be careful not to step on each other's toes, though. This can be a very good long-term thing and a very possible marriage.

Capricorn Man

There is definitely something that inspires Sagittarius woman's interest in Capricorn man. He's intelligent, interesting, stable, and pretty much knows what he wants. Strangely enough, too, he exposes her sensitive side—something she doesn't show to many. In this case, though, it makes her feel oddly vulnerable. In fact, these two are cut from different cloths. Sagittarius woman feels and goes with instinct, while Capricorn man rationalizes. In bed, he normally does not have the fire or the passion to fill her with the emotions she craves. This is a very possible long-term thing, but it's not a probable marriage.

Aquarius Man

Aquarius and Sagittarius are strangely drawn to each other. The chemistry here can be powerful and wicked. Know one thing, though. Life isn't fair. Sexually, the two reach new heights. Emotionally and mentally, however, these two will eventually have big problems. Aquarius analyzes and thinks. Sagittarius wants affection, though she won't ask for it. Ironically enough, though this can be a very promising long-term thing, it's not a probable (or long-lasting) marriage.

ESSENTIAL

They can travel together and have new experiences, but Sagittarius woman will soon regard Aquarius man as emotionally distant and maybe even superficial, at times. True, these two are some of the more independent and liberal of the signs. But their common ground stops there.

Pisces Man

Others see these two as complete opposites. She's a little more macho than he is, yet still very feminine— nurturing and romantic, for instance—and sophisticated. In other words, she's a strong woman. However, he gives her the respect and the power she craves so this may even be a good match.

 FACT

Sagittarius man and Pisces woman is the ultimate combination. But Sagittarius woman and Pisces man can work, too. Quiet strength between these two is the ultimate factor. And they seem to bring out the best in one another.

True, if he has no Fire in his chart, he may be a little too sweet for her in bed. But if she's smart (which she is) and if she cares, she can bring out the reckless, stronger side of Pisces. If he decides to be loyal to her and gives out some Fire, this can be a long-term relationship. It's also a very possible marriage.

Aries Man

Fire. Fire. Fire. Aries man tempts Sagittarius woman like crazy. He's got her, and she knows it (even if she doesn't let on). She loves his unpredictability, his nerve, his sex appeal, and the fact that he's outright ballsy. She admires him for the way he so easily deals with people and always knows the right thing to say. Unfortunately, when she gets to understand him better, she sees him as a showoff and someone who doesn't necessarily keep his word. They like to experiment in bed, and Aries will make Sagittarius feel completely cherished. This alone will get her, though she may suffer some disappointment in the future when his interests quickly turn off and on again. Most likely, she's more evolved and mature than he is. This pair can still be very possible, whether for a long-term relationship or for marriage.

Taurus Man

Taurus man sparks Sagittarius woman's interest because she really likes the way he looks—well built, sexy, and powerful. She's instinctively drawn to him sexually, and these two can move mountains in bed. Taurus man pays homage to Sagittarius. He worships her (services her!) and she, in turn, knows what a treasure she's found. Unfortunately, Sagittarius is way too liberal and independent for conservative Taurus. He'll want security and trust—which she can give him—but, most likely, he won't wait long enough. If Taurus gets totally obsessed with Sagittarius, which he's prone to do, she may give him a chance. This can be a possible long-term relationship. It's also a possible marriage, just probably not a good one.

 ALERT!

> Taurus will shy away from conflict, and when the two argue he misses the crux of the matter, the subtleties. This drives Sagittarius woman up the wall.

Gemini Man

Gemini makes Sagittarius smile and laugh. In fact, he also makes her feel . . . deeply. And this is a problem. Though Gemini appears sensitive and sensuous, he's really not half as emotionally driven as Sagittarius woman. This is dangerous. She wants to conquer him—to make him *feel*. In bed, Gemini brings out the wildness of Sagittarius. She wishes they truly connected more. This can be a very possible long-term thing, but it's not a probable marriage.

Cancer Man

This is a tossup. It really depends how mature Cancer man is. If he knows himself and can voice his emotions, this can work. Cancer man can sometimes gain security by playing the Casanova with women. But when he sees Sagittarius woman, he gets inspired. He wants to win her, and she just may let him. In bed, they become incredibly adventurous if Sagittarius can make him think he's completely in charge. Remember, he's a Cardinal sign (meaning he likes to dominate.) No matter, she's instinctive enough to let him take the reins. This relationship can flourish only if Sagittarius gets to the bottom of who Cancer really is. He'll sidestep and hide from her scrutinizing gaze. If he lets her in, though, and if she's truly ready to settle down, this can be a good long-term thing. It's a good marriage, too.

Leo Man

Ouch. These two have a hard time getting together. Why? Believe it or not, their sexual craving for each other is so strong that talk is pretty much impossible. Also, both have a quiet side, with each failing to voice how they truly feel. Sagittarius woman thinks Leo man is just toying with her, but this is simply an act. In fact, he's probably dead serious about her. They misinterpret and misunderstand that, really, the love is mutual. Most likely, Sagittarius will put it out there and wait for Leo man to come back strong and steady with verbal cues. But he's action-oriented, like Sagittarius woman. In bed, Leo whispers endearments Sagittarius has wanted to hear her entire life. And the physical side of things is perfect. If they can let go of their ideals, they can have a long, passionate, wonderful relationship. This can be a probable long-term thing and a very possible marriage.

ESSENTIAL

> There can be two problems here. One, Sagittarius needs to let Leo man dominate in bed completely. And two, Leo man, due to his insecurity, will not show or verbalize his feelings often. Trust is essential for Sagittarius. Leo doesn't stay unless he's smitten.

Virgo Man

Sagittarius woman is completely taken aback by Virgo's freshness. His wit and self-mocking humor get to her. She likes it. She also understands his abrupt way of dealing with people—she does it sometimes, too. But, strangely enough, she can't stand his intolerance of so many things. Unfortunately, this leads to trouble in the bedroom. Sagittarius loses just a bit a respect for Virgo man only because they have two completely different ways of seeing things. She sparks his interest in a physical way—but that's all. These two might have a long-term thing, but it's not probable. Marriage isn't likely either.

Libra Man

Sagittarius has got it bad for Libra. She senses a troubled soul—one whom she can save. She's right about the first part. He may have problems, but she's not likely the one who can rescue him. Actually, Libra sees her as too brash and bold for his tastes. He'd like to match her step for step . . . for at least one night, but not much more than that. If he goes to bed with her, it can be all sparks, but Sagittarius may just wake up the next morning, perhaps, regretting their liaison— which Libra might do, too. These two are perfectly friendship-friendly, but they aren't love-bound. All in all, this may be an okay long-term thing, but it's not a probable marriage.

Scorpio Man

If Sagittarius woman was looking for someone cool, a real challenge, she's finally met her match. Dark, mysterious, sexy Scorpio gets her going, and he's enthralled by her, too. When does she fall in love with Scorpio man? After she goes to bed with him. They fit together perfectly. However, Scorpio is much more pessimistic than optimistic Sagittarius. He brings her down with his moody, self-pitying ways. She also provokes him to defend himself—which he detests. If Scorpio is mature and has his temper under control, though, this can work. It depends on how much the two are willing to give passion and love a real chance. If they are, this can be a possible long-term thing and a possible marriage beyond that.

Love Planets: Venus and Mercury

Even if all the signs in your chart are Earth or even Air, a bit of Sagittarius will still give you an expansive, generous, fun-loving side. Sagittarius can even make conservative Taurus or Capricorn more liberal. Freedom to travel and learn new trades is an interest Sagittarius can't deny. And because Sagittarius is a renaissance man (or woman), you'll probably be good at everything you pour your heart into. Needless to say, Sagittarius is a positive, fiery sign to have light up your chart. Read on to learn some of the aspects.

 FACT

> Like Scorpio, Sagittarius has a bit of a dark side, too. If your Venus is in Sagittarius, you're likely to experience some self-pity. You also tend to be harsh in your judgment of others and scathingly self-critical. Try to relax, and give yourself and others a break.

Venus in Sagittarius

You crave adventure, intense experiences, wild, passionate sex, and all-or-nothing love. Sexually charged, you recognize attraction and desire in an instant. In love, you usually get what you want, when you want it. Some say you're irresistible. Before you commit yourself to a relationship, you need to be convinced. You'll never settle for something or someone less than what you think is right for you. In fact, when you're really in love, you give all—though you're not clingy or too possessive. When you're not, you're a heartbreaker. You're honest in relationships, generous, and more sensitive than you'd like others to see. Venus in Sagittarius pairs well with Venus in Leo, Sagittarius, Pisces, Aries, and Gemini.

Mercury in Sagittarius

You may switch subjects too rapidly for other people's tastes, but that's because so many different topics fascinate you. You especially love to talk about foreign cultures and countries, the subtleties of language, travel, adventure, sports—doing them, not watching—and the intricacies of love and sex. You're funny, and you like to laugh. You're faithful only when you're really in love. You don't get along with people unless they truly appreciate irony, sarcasm, and your particular brand of humor. If someone doesn't get you, you try to explain yourself, but you won't waste too much time doing it. Instead, you're off following more worthwhile pursuits. You're a natural-born flirt but, oddly enough, you connect extremely well with babies, children, even animals, sometimes, more than you do with people. Mercury in Sagittarius links well with Mercury in Aries, Sagittarius, Leo, Capricorn, Gemini, Pisces, and Cancer.

Chapter 10
Capricorn

Capricorn is always a fascinating type, not so easy to know profoundly. In fact, you'll have to dig deep to get to the heart of Capricorn. Here are some tried-and-true tips about the real Capricorn. In this chapter, discover his whole reason for being, and find out his life's desires.

The Strong, Silent One

Capricorn seems easy to figure out. True, he can be predictable on some points. But at other times, he'll come out and surprise you. One thing every Capricorn concedes is that he knows himself well. This may be correct, yes. But he (and you) may also be shocked about what interests and excites him! (From this chapter, you may even know before he does.) He has strong convictions about what he's looking for in a mate—in this, yes, he has clear ideas. But even Capricorn can be swayed.

 ESSENTIAL

Capricorns are ten times slyer than you'd imagine (and much more so than Virgo and Taurus, the other Earth signs). They'll put a kernel of an idea into your head and then watch, wait, and see what you do with it. In fact, they'll do this repeatedly until they believe they understand you.

Capricorn likes to analyze and formulate. Without a plan, he feels bereft. In other words, he's not likely to "wing it." But Capricorn goes more for a specific character type with certain moral ideas than for a certain look or body type. In love, he'll want a strong, vivacious partner he can be proud of. In truth, he's no wallflower himself. He may hide behind his scruples and ideals, but he also can be a lot more easygoing than he looks. He's always got something to say, and he doesn't freely give his approval right off the bat. Instead, he'll hand you a rope and let you hang yourself with it.

The Orderly and Cautious Soul

Most Capricorns tend to be orderly, but get this: They categorize people as well. In other words, besides keeping their houses relatively spic-and-span, Capricorn desperately wants to label you, put you in a marked box and stick you on the shelf along with other classified would-be mates. Truthfully, she's not okay simply getting to know a three-dimensional you. She's very cautious about giving her heart, and she's likely to stereotype you to some degree before you two even make it out of the starting gate. You're either this way or that. And once Capricorn has "figured you out," she's not likely to change her mind so quickly or to tailor her "hard-won" results.

True, this can be tedious or even offensive, but here's a little secret: If you say and do all the "right" things in the beginning, you'll have Capricorn convinced he knows you. And since he's not likely to change his mind quickly on how he perceives anything—remember, he's a cardinal sign (he likes being "right")—you need only act the part in the very beginning. And then you're free to be you! How does that sound? Find out Capricorn's mode of operation, and it's smooth sailing from there. (Note, too, that if you've already started a relationship with Capricorn, and you already have a little piece of his heart, it's not too late to take the advice of this chapter.)

Emotional Power

It's sad to see that Capricorn gets a bad reputation for being cold, though. She's anything but. The truth is that Capricorn will hold onto the reins until she knows she can trust you. She also wants to make sure you two are on the same page. Sure, she's not likely to dive into a love situation; if she does, nine times out of ten she has someone in the wings as emotional backup. But when and if she decides it's you, you're likely to have her heart served to you on a silver, gold, or platinum platter.

The Inner Child

Inside of Capricorn man lurks a little boy he doesn't like to show. You can bring this out of him. Make him laugh at himself and the world around him, say things that will impress him, and he's likely to make you the goddess of his heart (this is the same with Capricorn woman). He'll do anything to win and keep you. What needs to come across here is that you're not a capricious, whimsical, too-free-spirit type who's likely to hang him emotionally out to dry or to drop money too easily. (He'll prompt you and poke you to say that you are! Don't fall into this trap!)

Capricorn is always attracted to this breath of fresh air; for instance, Capricorn is instinctively enamored by generous, expensive-tasted, big-hearted Leo, but he will intuitively fear this kind of person at the same time. In fact, he will do his best not to get too emotionally involved because he senses that the combo will not work. Why? He hates to fail. Will it? No. Not if you know how to put yourself in the best light and show off your greatest assets.

 FACT

Capricorn is definitely not stingy. However, he's also not necessarily the financial whiz that most astrologers make him out to be. No matter. Even though his funds may be modest, Capricorn is still likely to be interested in financial security.

The Critical Capricorn

Like Virgo, Capricorn almost always takes himself too seriously. He's self-mocking at times and deliberately critical. In fact, he's likely to father you; telling you what you need to do and how you need to do it. You can stand up to Capricorn, but don't defend yourself. You must make sure you let him know that yes, he's right, and that you will immediately make the appropriate changes. If you don't, Capricorn will think you have your own agenda—one that doesn't agree with his. He will never appreciate this about you the way other independent cardinal signs like Aries or Libra would. Capricorn needs to dominate—especially Capricorn man. So let Capricorns in general think they're in charge—especially with money issues.

ESSENTIAL

> The juxtaposition here is that Capricorn—man or woman, alike—wants a vulnerable, soft mate who will be dependent and reliable at the same time . . . emotionally and financially.

The Art of Attraction

Above all, Capricorn wants assurance should he falter. He does want emotional security, but one stereotype is true: All Capricorns need to know their love partnerships are also covered financially at all times. But what many astrologers fail to see is that the buck literally stops here. It bears repeating that not every Capricorn is good at making mountains of money. He only really needs to know that things can be paid for. This, indeed, is incredibly important to him, even if Capricorn makes it seem like it's not.

The Long Haul

Yet, Capricorn devotes his love, heart and soul, when he's sure of you. He's very linked with family. Actually, Capricorn is a real provider—Capricorn man, especially. He'll want to be the major breadwinner. In fact, he can be a bit adamant about living off the money he, and only he, makes. Insecure Capricorns, though they try to hide it—will be dead set on proving to you that they can support you completely, in terms of work, home, and finances.

Capricorn, regardless of whether or not she's close to her family, is not likely to move to a different country or even another county on a moment's notice. She tends to stay close to home base or at least take the time to decide on a big move. Also, Capricorn will stick around even when a relationship is less than stellar. Sure, she'll complain to her friends and family and even warn you that she's on her way out, but it will take a lot just for her to walk away without looking back (not unlike Taurus). This is true of all Capricorns. Like Aries, they hate the thought that they might be "missing out" and they also simply can't stand teary goodbye scenes.

He/She: The Little Stuff Counts

Capricorn, it should be said, is also almost always conservative in nature. He very much appreciates an out-there, gaudy, sensual, and sexy look, but he's more likely to be drawn to the tried-and-true: a nice suit or tailored pants with pearls, or a dignified button-down with pants and good (comfortable but expensive) shoes.

 FACT

Even if Capricorn is a born pessimistic, she's not naive. What you may call negative, she'll call realistic. This goes for clothing, too. She admires a man who knows how to dress for the occasion.

Resourceful and Inspiring

There's something incredibly inspiring about Capricorn. Her personality is so polished, even if her clothes aren't always. She's smart—like an international sponge. She soaks up all kinds of information and spews it out on a moment's notice. She's incredibly resourceful, too. And she's got a big heart—for the pursuits and people she deems worthy.

 ALERT!

> Just make sure not to get on the wrong side of Capricorn. Quietly and carefully, he'll sneak up on you—instinctively knowing how to push your buttons. And he has a fantastic memory . . . he can reach back decades into his bottomless memory to find something to throw back at you.

In truth, you need only win a Capricorn's affection to see the fiery, beautiful, sweet soul lurking underneath. With friends and in love, Capricorn woman and Capricorn man are equally unlikely to wear their hearts on their sleeves. But if they really respect you and dub you a "worthwhile cause," you may feel like royalty—because they'll treat you that way. They're more givers than takers, generous rather than parsimonious.

Pillow Talk: Signs in the Bedroom

Surprisingly enough, Capricorn doesn't mind some aggressiveness on your part—at least to get the ball rolling. In fact, he'll probably welcome it. But Capricorn isn't the verbal lover Gemini or Aries or even Sagittarius may be. Actually, he's more likely to joke just to break the tension (and for emotional protection) than to spew out words of love, passion, and dreams of forever after.

The Secret Capricorn Man

Capricorn man is a sought-after candidate for long-term commitment. He worships his family and works hard to take care of everyone around him. He also makes a fantastic father. Capricorn, in bed, can sometimes be a hard nut to crack—depending on the individual. He can hold back; it may even seem that he likes—no, favors—the traditional positions. But when he lets go, his tastes vary across the board. Capricorn men are the first to hide their more "out there" ideas of sex until they really feel comfortable with you. Even then, they may still choose concealment. They have to admit things to themselves, and here lies the true crux of the problem.

Capricorn man may sometimes keep his sexual fantasies bottled up. You can get them out of him, perhaps, by acting shy or inexperienced (even if you're just role-playing). Try playing the virgin—Capricorn will eat it up. In this sense, Virgo woman is actually a good choice for Capricorn man. You can be seductive and aggressive to get him into bed, but once there, let Capricorn take over. Remember, he likes to dominate. He needs to feel like the he-man, the protector.

 ESSENTIAL

> Most Capricorn men are not big talkers after the act. Whatever you do, do not analyze or comment about the sex unless it's high praise for him! Capricorn is sensitive, thin-skinned when it comes to his masculine pride!

The Secret Capricorn Woman

Like her male counterpart, Capricorn woman is smart with a capital "S." She can be crafty, too. If she's got it in her mind that she's getting a man into bed, she won't have much trouble with it. If you want to seduce her, there are a few things you can do. Though these may seem stereotypical or over the top, they'll still work. In order to capture Capricorn woman, assure her of at least four of the following six things:

- She comes before your friends.
- You understand the way the world works.
- You know people who can help her get ahead with her career and in life.
- You have sincere feelings for her.
- You're not the least bit stingy.
- You'll be there for her emotionally and financially.

This may make Capricorn woman sound opportunistic or even a little superficial. She's not. She sincerely wants to feel a bond with you—and these things may help her feel more comfortable. From her sheer practical nature, these traits are important to her. Never lie about anything, though. Capricorn can't stand a liar. She's straightforward about herself, so you need to be, too. Jewelry, compliments, and flowers also work well for Capricorn woman but the most important gift you can give her is the knowledge that your love for her is real.

Sun Love Matches

Here is what's important to all Capricorns: security, intelligence, a quick sense of humor, financial know-how, street smarts, mental stability (capricious folks need not apply), self-confidence, and the ability to give more emotionally than they, themselves, are giving. Capricorn is always attracted to the breezy freshness of Air signs, but this is not always the best partner for him. Romantically, he gets along well with Fire signs, though other Earth signs may have the same ideals in life. Read on to learn about the love matches for Capricorn woman.

Capricorn Man

These two have the same ideas about how things should be done. They know how to build a future together the "correct" way (according to their standards) and this seems to work. But a couple of problems come with this union. First, they beat each other to the punch line—since they think so alike, the surprise factor is ruled out. Also, when left to themselves in conversation, they can get as serious as a funeral. If one of them has many Air signs, this won't be a problem, though. Sexually, two Capricorns can be either soul mates in bed or partners who rub each other the wrong way (literally and figuratively). All in all, this relationship can be heavy. With Air signs in either of their charts, though, this can be a long-term thing and a possible marriage.

 FACT

There are two types of Capricorn: the pessimist and the idealist. They're complete opposites. For a Capricorn union to work, the two types must come together. In this case, opposites do not attract.

Aquarius Man

It's such a shame these two have their differences. If they could solve them, they'd get along great. Chances are, Capricorn woman will be the one to end it if it gets to the point of stay or go. Aquarius is intelligent, interesting, fun, and crazy about Capricorn woman. But even so, Aquarius man probably can't be what she needs and wants. He puts his friends before her. He has spending habits that drive Capricorn woman mad. The truth is, though, there can be real love here. If these two can get it together, this can be a very possible long-term relationship. It's a possible marriage if Aquarius chooses to give Capricorn what she's looking for.

Pisces Man

Sorry to say, these two don't go together. There may be attraction but that's where it probably ends. Pisces gets annoyed at Capricorn's know-it-all attitude. He admires her intelligence but wonders about her street smarts. Also, Capricorn can break Pisces' idealistic bubble. She's a troublemaker, he thinks, as he heads for the hills. Pisces is also sensitive to Capricorn's criticism and may think she's a bit too tough for him. In bed, they can have an interesting liaison if he wows Capricorn sufficiently in all other areas. Then she'll let him dominate. This is not a probable long-term thing and not a likely marriage, either.

Aries Man

Aries man has enough passion, fire, and stamina for the both of them. Capricorn woman doesn't necessarily trust his jump-into-love ways but she lets him woo her. Chances are, though, she may not have the patience Aries needs when he acts the little boy. If Capricorn is not careful, she'll unwittingly insult him, and he'll change his mind about her quickly. In bed, this can be a fiery affair. If there's anyone who can open up Capricorn, it's Aries. This can be a possible long-term thing. It's not a probable marriage, but it's not impossible, either.

ESSENTIAL

> Instinctively, Capricorn woman doesn't believe Aries will be the secure rock she's looking for in life—and she's probably right. But he thrills her all the same.

Taurus Man

There's a sexual thing going on here, though, truthfully, Capricorn knows far too well how to get Taurus to do exactly as she wishes. This may ruin the fun for a Capricorn woman who wants to play, but it's a big turn-on for the Capricorn woman who's looking for a secure partner. When it comes to money, Capricorn woman is the Bull's ultimate fantasy. Though he spends it in odd places (ones that she probably doesn't agree with), he's still generous with her, and she appreciates that. This can be one hot sexual fling, but Capricorn may not trust Taurus's feelings for the long term. This can, however, be a possible long-term thing, maybe even a marriage.

Gemini Man

Of all the Air signs, this one is least likely to bring out the best in Capricorn woman. Though they can have a nice flirt together, they're likely to have little else in common beyond a good sense of humor and an attraction. Capricorn's brand of humor is a little more sarcastic, subtle, or ironic. Gemini amuses Capricorn, but that's probably it. However, they can have fabulous sex and maybe even an affair that lasts—until one of them starts talking marriage. This can be a possible long-term thing. It's also possibly a marriage if Gemini has tons of Earth in his chart—but only if.

Cancer Man

It's interesting. These two recognize the good within each other. In other words, they like each other as people. They can have conversations on everything (though Cancer may be more closed-minded than even practical Capricorn). Cancer, sometimes, may even enjoy provoking Capricorn—getting a reaction from her by making her angry. Capricorn is so cool, so calm and collected. These two signs both prefer to have the upper hand. In bed, they take turns. In fact, this is probably the best thing in their relationship: wildness, fun, adventure, and even kinkiness (if Capricorn's willing). This is a possible long-term thing and marriage.

 ALERT!

> When these two fight, get out of the way! Do not get involved in the kind of maneuvers they pull on each other. Each will try to get you to help them or find out information. One word: *don't*.

Leo Man

Leo and Capricorn can get along so well. Mentally, they're made for each other. Capricorn woman inspires Leo to be the best he can be; meanwhile, she compliments him and strokes his ego. The one thing she doesn't understand about Leo is that he can be insecure at times. He's not as strong as he seems. She can also be insensitive to his feelings, overly critical at times. Leo admires Capricorn's sense of humor, intelligence, and her all-around interesting personality. Truthfully, though, these two can have a hard time of it in bed. Both are too quiet for the other's tastes. Leo wants gushing words that Capricorn can't provide. He also wants more drama and fire in the bedroom and Capricorn tends to stay away from drama. All in all, this can definitely be a long-term thing and even a possible marriage, though it's not recommended.

Virgo Man

Chances are, Virgo man just doesn't give the kind of emotional attention Capricorn woman needs and secretly hopes for. She may seem like a pessimist, but she genuinely wishes Virgo would turn around and worship the ground she walks on. When it comes to money, finances, starting up new businesses, and planning for the future, no one impresses Capricorn the way Virgo man does. Sexually, Capricorn can feel when Virgo's holding back. She wonders why he's so secretive about his sexual habits. If Virgo is willing to open up and Capricorn is too, though, it's a good long-term thing with a good chance for marriage.

Libra Man

Strangely enough, this can be a very positive union. Libra brings out Capricorn's fun, happy side and, in turn, Capricorn gives Libra the kind of emotional security he's looking for. If she's a soft Capricorn, so much the better. Sexually, Libra can inspire Capricorn to try new things. Capricorn knows deep down she's always wanted to experiment, but she'll never let on. Therefore, Libra will feel like a master in the bedroom. This can work. It's a very possible long-term relationship and also a probable marriage.

 FACT

Libra is a cardinal sign and wants to lead. Capricorn does, too, but if she's in love, she'll know how to handle him.

Scorpio Man

Sexually, Scorpio knows how to rouse Capricorn . . . face it, Scorpio knows how to rouse anyone. Instinctively, Scorpio can feign innocence, all the while pulling out Capricorn's secrets without her knowing it. He's smart in this aspect, and hopefully he won't discover any skeletons he's not willing to deal with. The same is true of Capricorn. She'll dissect, analyze, and try to get to the heart of Scorpio. This actually may be a case of two wrongs not making a right, because they're too similar at times. They're likely to have a very strong attraction, so this can be a possible long-term thing, but it's not a likely marriage.

 QUESTION?

What's another thing these two have in common?
Oddly enough, it's collecting knickknacks. It's possible Capricorn and Scorpio share hobbies: antique shopping, restoring old furniture, or hunting down strange kitchen utensils. Though they're both neat, this side of them gives the term "pack rat" new meaning.

Sagittarius Man

If Sagittarius is born closer to Scorpio cusp or in the middle of Sagittarius and Capricorn, these two have less of a chance. A Sagittarius bordering Capricorn is likely to interest Capricorn woman more. However, these two have truly different ways of operating. If a particular Sagittarius man needs more security than most others, though, Capricorn woman can be a perfect match (especially if he has a love of money). Sexually, Capricorn recognizes Sagittarius for the talented lover he is, and Sagittarius's down-to-earth side feels a natural bond with Capricorn's earthy, sexual bent. If he's very attracted to her, he can win her love. If not, she may just go to bed with him simply for curiosity's sake. This can be a positive long-term thing with maybe even marriage in the future.

Love Planets: Venus and Mercury

If you've got Capricorn in the rest of your chart, it will make you weigh out pluses and minuses before committing. When you make a pledge, though, you're more than likely to honor it. Venus in Capricorn, for example, tends to take love very seriously and is not likely to cheat on a partner. A certain inherent wisdom comes with the sign of Capricorn, too. Below, discover what Capricorn means to the rest of your personality.

Venus in Capricorn

Dedicated, loving, and loyal, Venus in Capricorn can be the most finicky in love. But when you commit, you're a wonderful partner. Though you may be extra critical of your mate, you do it out of love. Unfortunately, many partners aren't willing to accept this. A person needs to be thick-skinned to deal with the likes of you. You also change between being idealistic and practical, romantic and matter-of-fact. You're a tough nut to crack, and many wonder if they'll actually dig you all the way out of your shell. Venus in Capricorn goes well with Taurus, Leo, Capricorn, Virgo, Libra, and (sometimes) Aquarius.

Mercury in Capricorn

A fast talker, that's what you are, but only when you feel like it. You can be wildly antisocial, at times. You always seem to find the one big interest of the person you're talking to. Though you have zero patience for ignorance and flights of fancy, you can amuse yourself talking with almost anyone—even if you can't dredge up an ounce of respect for the person. You don't even bother trying to be overly nice. Though you're not particularly nasty, it goes against your code of ethics to be fake to someone you don't like. Instead, you're more likely to say hello and then head the other way. It's important to you that people listen to what you're saying. Mercury in Capricorn goes well with Mercury in Capricorn, Libra, Leo, Taurus (maybe), Sagittarius, Virgo, and Aquarius.

Chapter 11
Aquarius

Remember the Broadway show or the hit movie *Hair*? It's the Age of Aquarius we're talking about: freedom and liberty; being you and being loved for it; adoring the unusual, the strange, even the wacky. These are all real traits of the slippery Aquarius. How do you win his heart? Read on.

The Eclectic

Nine times out of ten, Aquarius will throw you for a loop. He seems so attentive, so interested, so curious about you. You feel so special with him. Guess what? It's possible he's like this with everyone. But it's also possible you're the one, and you need to know the difference. Aquarius loves being entertained and amused. The world—including the people in it—is his oyster, and breaking people down is his art. Aquarius gets bored easily. He needs constant stimulus.

The Friendship Sign

Yes, this is the friendship sign. Yet, strangely enough, many astrologers fail to mention that Aquarius can be actively antisocial when he feels like it. This has more to do with the company than with how he feels about himself, though, distinguishing Aquarius from the other antisocial signs (like Scorpio or Cancer). If Aquarius even senses he'll have fun with you or a "different" kind of evening, he'll be dressed and out the door in a jiffy, ready for the night ahead.

 ESSENTIAL

Aquarius has so many fans! They all relate to her in some way, and she's always nice to everyone. Therefore, she tends to attract undesirables—people with whom she wouldn't mind *not* being friends, but who remain acquaintances nevertheless.

Higher Beings

You're not likely to find an Aquarius who isn't spiritual. Even if she seems practical at heart, she still believes if only a little (and actually more than she wants to) in a higher force—or destiny. The strange, the mystical, the odd and wonderful will always inspire Aquarius to dream a little dream. And though not every Aquarius knows how to tap into her instinctual, psychic side, this doesn't mean she doesn't have one.

 QUESTION?

Does Aquarius get attached?
Of course! It just takes more than sex, attraction, good conversation, and financial security to get them involved. Aquarians see the big picture. If you're part of their future: absolutely.

True, Aquarius has the power to emotionally distance himself more than any other sign. And he is able to control what he shows to others. Even if Aquarius is dying inside of love, he'll make light of it. What you see, then, is the product of someone who is very good at talking to and convincing himself. But don't be fooled—Aquarius is no dummy. He knows the one way to keep a partner coming back: tranquility. No other sign can remain as calm when a love mate is on the verge of leaving. Though he may have his temporary outbursts, he knows how to reel a partner in by being cool and collected.

The Art of Attraction

Just what is it that attracts Aquarius? He'll say, "I know it when I see it." In fact, the only constant in Aquarius's liaisons is that each partner is unique. Are you a showoff? Do you flaunt your money, car, or nice clothing? Aquarius couldn't care less. He goes for sure self-confidence, a quiet arrogance, and something or someone he's not sure of. Yes, Aquarius wants a bit of a challenge. But if you're too much of a challenge, he won't waste his time like a Fire sign would. Strike a balance.

 ALERT!

> Aquarius doesn't trust people who frequently compliment him! Use your praise sparingly, when you really mean it. He'll appreciate it more.

The Long Haul

Though Aquarius can be very instinctive, he's actually the most naive of all the signs. Why? He trusts everyone. And he always roots for the person he believes is the underdog, even if that's not the true case at all. In other words, even if the "underdog" is snowing him under, Aquarius will quickly rise to the occasion and take this individual under his wing. For those who know semipractical Aquarius, it's hard to understand how he can be so gullible. Why doesn't he see through those preying on his good nature?

But Aquarius is always sought after, and for a reason. She doesn't have a set rule of conduct. Instead, each situation is new territory. She can make an excellent parent, one who shows her child acceptance, no matter what. As a matter of fact, children of Aquarius parents learn to be independent at a very early age. Aquarius parents trust their progeny and let them do pretty much what they want, while letting them know, still, that they love them deeply.

 QUESTION?

Is Aquarius faithful?
Here's a simplified answer: Only when she's really in love and can see a future with someone. If not, the answer is no, not ever. (The only barely possible exception might be if she has her Venus in Cancer, Pisces, Capricorn, or Taurus.)

He/She: The Little Stuff Counts

Aquarius is not necessarily into glamour. He knows how to dress down, and he's far too practical to dress up for a barbeque. Actually, there is an androgynous theme that presents itself many times with Aquarius. Some Aquarius women are tomboys, and some Aquarius men have a feminine side. It depends on the person. But Aquarius likes to shock people. He does it for fun.

Sexiness Is What Counts

Aquarius looks for an innate sexiness in a love partner. It doesn't really matter how you dress, as long as you come off cool, collected, and not clumsy in the least. Actually, Aquarians usually go for a less conservative genre of dress (people, too). Aquarius woman is attracted to masculine, he-man earthy types, and Aquarius men like natural, feminine types who wear little or no makeup. Don't even think of playing the traditional housewife/husband. Aquarius has no use for you if you're just trying to impress or if you're typical or mundane.

Pillow Talk: Signs in the Bedroom

One word here: Grab! Aquarius is impressed by bold, outrageous moves. You can seduce her before you've even won her heart. Just keep in mind that Aquarius, more than any other sign in the zodiac, can absolutely separate love from sex. She will sleep with whomever, wherever, whenever she wants. No compunction, no regrets.

 ESSENTIAL

Aquarius never goes for shy partners. She instinctively looks for people who can dominate her. This is even true of Aquarius men, to a degree. Aquarius always needs to look up to a partner.

But sex is very important to Aquarius. You can make Aquarius fall in love in this way. He'll get used to you, addicted to you if you see him over a period of time. This is an excellent way to sneak up on Aquarius. Before you know it, you'll have him. And he'll be yours, too.

The Secret Aquarius Man

Bright, lively, fascinating even, this man can get you to talk—and how! Here is where you need to be extra careful. Aquarius man looks for a few things in a love mate. He'll be friendly and gregarious, but all the while, he's watching for warning signs. He knows what he doesn't want. Look at the following list. If you give Aquarius an idea that you are any of these things, he will run the other way:

- Needy
- Clingy
- Neurotic in any way
- Lacking a good group of friends
- Too possessive
- Insecure
- A wallflower
- A hawk, in terms of your politics (Aquarius wants peace)
- Not interested in travel

Friends are important to Aquarius man. If you try to rule his life, or tell him not to go out too much, he'll do exactly the opposite of what you say.

 FACT

Aquarius man wants to see the world a better place. Show him you're interested in saving the planet, charity, animals, and/or starving children. Mass-produced items (including designer brand names) are, according to him, bourgeois. He will need to know your ideals mirror his own.

Aquarians are born rebels. They live to go against the grain. They need to learn something new every day and can't stand to be bored. If you want an Aquarius man, let him win you. Show him you've got a life, a million things that interest you, and let him know you know how wonderful you are. He'll catch on.

The Secret Aquarius Woman

This woman has more fans than any of the other signs. People are drawn to her. Men are attracted to her. Why? She seems so down-to-earth, so tranquil and caring. In truth, she does empathize with almost anyone. Put Aquarius in a room full of people where she doesn't belong, and she'll still come out having every person in the place wanting to be her friend. She can rub shoulders with the lot of them. She's a chameleon. And she's no snob—not ever.

 FACT

Aquarius woman *can* make love when she's not in love . . . she's just ten times more likely to "finish" when she is. Try as they do to go against the grain, Aquarian woman, to their dismay, actually do need to be in love to experience good lovemaking.

What interests her? The weird, the strange, the unusual—that's what. Take her to an ethnic restaurant, preferably one where you can sit on the floor on cushions. Eye contact is very important here. Seduce her with deep, sensual, sexy stares. Always be yourself, though. Aquarius can smell a fake from a mile away. Ask her what she wants—she'll tell you. Ask her what her fantasies are. She may just describe them to you. Get her to open up, and she'll feel more connected to you. That's the secret. You'll have her.

Sun Love Matches

If Aquarius has learned one thing in life, it's that he likes the unpredictable. Aquarians, themselves, are the most spontaneous creatures. Aquarius lives to say things to shock you, and he changes on a dime just to confuse you. He hates it when someone tries to figure him out. On the same note, though, Aquarius is immediately attracted to sensual, thinking Earth signs who balance out his sometimes overly cool, tranquil demeanor. Other Air signs interest him as well, but only if the intended has a bit of Earth in her chart. Otherwise, the two never get around to doing anything. Read on to discover the love matches for Aquarius woman.

Aquarius Man

This couple is wildfire. Each sets a match to the brush and waits to watch it explode. They egg each other on, provoking each other past a healthy limit. Actually, both are tranquil—at least, that's the appearance they create—and are simply waiting for the other to make a move. This can be a problem. They make each other jealous and ignore the big issues. To stay together, they need to confront the reality of the situation. Sexually, they're made for each other. If this is love, it can work. If it's not, these two will do more damage to one another than either imagined possible. All in all, the match is a positive long-term thing and a very possible marriage.

Pisces Man

"Ahhh, a poet," Aquarius woman thinks. But what she senses is the Water in him, something that she may lack herself. Strong feelings sometimes equal weakness for her. She's interested, though, in what he has to say. He's more powerful than she believes. If she gives him a chance, his strength will come out. In fact, he's just as crafty as she is.

 FACT

> There's something that probably doesn't click with Aquarius about Pisces. They're cut from different cloth. They like each other, but they don't necessarily trust each other.

Pisces will shy away from Aquarius in bed. She may be a handful for him. Maybe they can have a brief, fun fling. This is not a probable long-term thing (but not negative should it occur), and it's also not a probable marriage.

Aries Man

This is a possible union. Here's the rub: Aries man needs someone he can cuddle with. Though he's a strong he-man (which inevitably turns Aquarius on), he's also a big softie. Family is very important to Aries. He'll woo her and wow her at first with his wild, passionate declarations of love. But then he'll wonder if he can keep a real hold on her. She's not exactly begging to have children, settle down, and be his property. (Aries man is notorious for putting women in their place.)

 ALERT!

> Aquarius woman sometimes spreads herself too thin with too many friends, interests, and hobbies. Aries man is also the social butterfly who doesn't always finish what he starts, though he probably is very successful with his work. Their problem is finding time to be together.

Still, this can work if Aquarius woman is very in love with him. She knows how to get his attention and keep it. This is not a probable long-term thing or marriage, but it's possible.

Taurus Man

This is probably the best combination of the lot. Taurus is sensuous and daring, and he makes Aquarius laugh. She's intrigued by his down-to-earth, no-nonsense approach to life. He's got everything on the ball, and he inspires her to do the same for herself. She also senses he can take good care of her. For some reason, he actually brings out her mothering nature. In bed, the two make fireworks. Sensual Taurus brings Aquarius to new heights. Ironically, Taurus is very traditional, and Aquarius is not conventional in the least. This can tear Taurus apart. Possessive Taurus doesn't scare Aquarius one bit because he's not too clingy with her. He's independent too, which is a good combination for Aquarius. This is a good chance for a long-term relationship, and there is a very good outlook for marriage if Aquarius doesn't shock Taurus to the core (or try to rush him to the altar).

Gemini Man

Did we say "troublemakers"? Yes. These two cause confusion and chaos around them. Gemini man can convince Aquarius to do almost anything. She's game. He'll instigate, though, and she'll be the one to carry it through.

 ESSENTIAL

Both Aquarius and Gemini like to shine, and Aquarius gets miffed when the spotlight moves away from her. If he is prone to tantrums or little lies, she will not stay to see the finale.

Gemini man, however, is more wary about love with Aquarius than the other way around. He can be a little needier, too, than she can. Though he amuses her, she's not at all sure she trusts him. Ditto for Gemini. This can work if both are mature and ready for something real. It's a very possible long-term thing, potentially leading to marriage.

Cancer Man

Cancer inspires Aquarius to be the best she can be. Her work flourishes with him. He supports her emotionally, all the way. They laugh together, and Cancer loves her self-mocking, droll sense of humor. He loves the fact that she's outgoing. But this bothers him, too. He seriously worries if he can control her—and he's soon to find out that maybe he can't. In fact, Aquarius is probably not capable of giving Cancer the kind of security he needs. Sexually, these two can be creative, spontaneous, and more than willing. However, while this relationship can make for a long-term thing, it's not necessarily the best match for marriage. (Chances get better if Cancer is extremely secure with himself.)

 FACT

Both Aquarius and Cancer are very instinctive, but Cancer relies more on feeling and Aquarius rationalizes things away. This can be a problem when they fight. For things to work, Aquarius needs to trust Cancer and let him win.

Leo Man

It's hard to say what the attraction is here. In terms of chemistry, they're a powerful mix. Most likely, Leo man will want to attack Aquarius woman (sexually) right away. She stirs up something in him, and he'll need to show her how he feels—physically. Instead, she needs to talk in order to feel a connection. When Leo's quiet, she doesn't realize that he's shy or pensive. Instead, she imagines he's judging her. Leo is sometimes critical with Aquarius, it's true, and though it wouldn't bother anyone else, his perfect, precise style drives Aquarius nuts. Also, she needs to feel free. He secretly wants a loyal, faithful partner he can dominate. He'll find it tough with her. This can be a long-term thing, but it's not a likely marriage.

Virgo Man

Besides Taurus, this may just be the second best combination with Aquarius. He amazes her with his business savvy. Aquarius, who's not necessarily interested in marrying a millionaire, is still interested in financial security. Virgo can provide her with this and how. She admires him for his ambition—probably because she lacks it herself—and is proud of his accomplishments and far-out money making ideas. Virgo is very creative, both in work and in bed (once he lets go, anyway). His earthy sensuality awakens the sexual woman within. He lets her do what she wants, also. The only problem here is that Virgo is antisocial. This can work, though. They have a very good chance for a long-term thing and a good chance for marriage.

Libra Man

Believe it or not, Libra actually has a bigger libido than even Aquarius. He'll have her craving him before she's realized what happened. The problem here is indecision—a constant with Libra, but Aquarius brings it out in him more. He's not sure of her. She's not sure of him. They waver back and forth from being completely enamored to bickering like children.

 ESSENTIAL

> Libra hates to argue, but Aquarius challenges him, bringing everything out in the open—which is strange for Aquarius who normally waits until the last second to make waves.

Fortunately, Aquarius handles it with tact and directness—a lot better than Gemini would, for example. In bed, they talk, laugh, and furiously consume the oxygen around them, burning it up as they go. This can be a long-term relationship, leading to a possible marriage.

Scorpio Man

Scorpio doesn't trust Aquarius much. Aquarius trusts Scorpio even less. But this only happens after some time together. In the beginning, they're two peas in a pod. Aquarius knows how to handle moody Scorpio with her positive, breezy character. If anyone can pull him out of the doldrums, it's her. However, his stress weighs on her and sometimes affects her too much. It can be an unhealthy situation if Scorpio is not mentally balanced or somewhat spiritually evolved. The bedroom can be passionate and sexy if Aquarius isn't pushy. This is a possible long-term thing, but it's not a probable marriage.

Sagittarius Man

At first, Sagittarius can be attracted to Aquarius's eclectic style. They both love to travel, and they have tons to talk about. He also sees and senses the grounded part of her that not everyone notices. The fact that she's so interested in the world makes him like her. But love? Sagittarius is way more fiery and intoxicated by feelings than emotionally distant Aquarius. He wants to be nurtured and doted on, while she doesn't always have the patience. Instead, she expects him to service her—which he will do, at least for a while. Eventually, Sagittarius may come to believe he can't rely on her. Again, emotionally they may be on two separate planes. This can last for a little while. They make a short to long-term affair, but it's not a highly recommended marriage.

Capricorn Man

Of all the Earth signs for Aquarius, this one is the least adaptable. Capricorn is conservative at heart and practical. The way Aquarius goes on binges sometimes makes him batty. She spends. She likes to go out. She socializes. In this case, Capricorn absolutely needs to have control of the wallet. Aquarius doesn't get this. She'll do what she feels like doing. He criticizes her, then she defends herself and gets angry.

FACT

> Two things can make a Capricorn-Aquarius match work: They have to truly respect each other, and Capricorn must secretly admire Aquarius's "no fear" attitude to life. He may just stick around, hoping some of Aquarius's style will rub off on him!

Capricorn doesn't open himself up enough in bed for her. She can bring it out of him, though, if she's willing to go slow (not likely). Mentally, they can get along, but Capricorn may be wary of Aquarius's strange tastes. He could think her superficial. All in all, this is a positive union. It could be a long-term relationship, but there's a big "if" here for marriage—not likely, but possible.

Love Planets: Venus and Mercury

Aquarius is interested in anything and everything. A little Aquarius in your chart in your Venus and/or Mercury will instantly make you a curious cat. You'll want to understand how things work and why. This aspect also makes you friendly and eager to help people in situations less fortunate than your own. You trust easily—sometimes too much. Remember, Aquarius is a social sign. Even if your sun sign is a bit antisocial, Aquarius will always lighten up your personality. Read on for a more comprehensive outlook on this.

Venus in Aquarius

Sorry to say that this is one of the least faithful love signs of the zodiac. There is only one way Venus in Aquarius can be true to a partner: when he or she is in utter and complete love. Aside from that, you're able to separate yourself. Actually, you can't help it. But that doesn't bother you. Instead, it gives you the upper hand in every love relationship—because you're the challenge. Sex is very important to you. You need to feel loved completely before you can really let go in bed. Venus in Aquarius goes well with Venus in: Taurus, Virgo, Capricorn, Cancer, Libra, and Aries.

Mercury in Aquarius

You vary from being loquacious when you're interested in something to going silent when you're not. No one knows what's going to come out of your mouth. One thing, though, is that you're never vulgar. You have an inherent elegance that comes out in your speech, a basic goodness that's hard to deny. People want to talk to you and confide in you. You can put someone at ease with a few choice words. This is your gift. Though you may be an open person, you're very careful with what you say. You never want to pressure anyone because you don't like it when they do the same to you. Mercury in Aquarius pairs with Mercury in Gemini, Aquarius, Taurus, Virgo, Aries, Libra, Leo, and Scorpio.

Chapter 12
Pisces

Pisces is the most misunderstood sign of the zodiac. There is nothing "weak" about Pisces, as many astrologers claim. He's not wishy-washy in the least! Instead, he's the quiet, strong type, instinctive and smart. In this chapter, find out more about this powerful sign.

The Sage

Here is the problem. It's not easy to get to the real core of Pisces. He doesn't like to wear his heart on his sleeve, and he doesn't like to share all the thoughts that go through his always-racing, complex mind. He thinks before he speaks and ponders the world and everything in it. Pisces always has his goals in mind, even if he doesn't act on them. He's also not likely to come out and say what he wants. He'll test you. His technique is to go around a subject and let you fill in the blanks. That way, he can tell if you're for him. He'll sit quietly and let you convince him, or he'll lead you into a conversation and see how well you respond.

Personable, Clever, Intelligent

Pisces understands the world and all its different kinds of victims. In other words, a Pisces can be empathetic with any brand of misery or sadness—even if she's not sympathetic. She knows just what to say to make you feel great. She's smart all around. She can boost anyone's ego and lift anyone's spirits.

 ESSENTIAL

Pisces can sometimes come off as a snob. He's not, though. This is the persona he gives off. Many times, he's born with an air of elitism and a certain savoir-faire, an innate elegance. Don't try to change him. You won't succeed.

In business, she's an effective individual because she understands the heart of the matter and is able to affect the people she deals with. She's personable, intelligent, and clever. But she's never the weak soul she's portrayed to be—quite the opposite. She's slick as a cat and just as quick.

Savvy and Sassy

Many astrologers say that Pisces is a dreamer. Not true. Instead, Pisces is a dreamer with a goal in mind. Pisces knows where she wants to be, and she tries her best to get there. She's incredibly good at her work and sometimes doesn't get the credit she deserves because she does everything without complaining—and seemingly effortlessly. Don't be fooled by tranquil Pisces. She's on top of things—always. She handles all with grace and finesse, and it's a rare occasion when things aren't handed in on time. In fact, Pisces will always go that extra mile to make a presentation just right.

The Love Package

This savvy applies to a Pisces' love life as well. Yes, Pisces wants a real love—but the package is more important than the single attributes. Each Pisces is different—some care more about money or wealth than others, some care more about looks (though this is less of an essential factor for all Pisces), and some want a partner who will draw out their vibrant, sassy nature that lays dormant without the help of a good mate to bring it out.

But one thing's for sure: Pisces wants to marry for love above all else.

The Art of Attraction

Pisces, though, can be very practical. He instinctively knows if a love match will work or if it won't. He won't stay in a relationship if he doesn't believe it's going somewhere. Also, many aspects of the relationship have to be good before he'll be convinced. If a mate is not giving, generous, and loving with him, he's not going to be those things either. However, Pisces man differs in this regard from Pisces woman. Pisces woman tends to be stronger in terms of character—at least until Pisces man comes into his own and learns from his past errors in judgment.

 ESSENTIAL

While both Pisces men and women may worship a potential mate from afar, Pisces woman will do something about it. Pisces man, on the other hand, usually keeps quiet. He might even develop an unhealthy obsession if he doesn't try to solve the problem and capture his heart's desire.

The Long Haul

Pisces makes an extraordinarily good parent. There are only two problems. Pisces could, at times, emotionally distance herself from her children when she needs to take a break from the grind, and she is geared to put her mate above all others . . . including her own progeny. This is not the rule, and there can be exceptions, of course. Still, this tends to be a Pisces trait.

Pisces does live for love—the good kind. That is, Pisces wants real love. He wants a partner who is a lover, best friend, and an equal. This, too, makes Pisces an excellent choice for a long-term mate. One thing to keep in mind, though, is that Pisces also needs a good creative outlet in which to express himself. Though he'll dedicate himself to a love partner and do everything in his power to make her feel nearly worshipped, he'll still need some kind of work or hobby (even if it's just reading) that will enable him to use his mind. Pisces has a fantastic imagination, and he doesn't like to let it stagnate for long.

He/She: The Little Stuff Counts

While Pisces woman is practically born refined and sophisticated, Pisces man can run the gamut from refined to bohemian to trendy. Though Pisces may seem like a snob from the outset, she is actually not so judgmental and is always diplomatic.

 FACT

Actually, because Pisces is a feminine sign, Pisces man can sometimes have effeminate qualities or, at the very least, a sympathetic ear. One physical attribute present in a Pisces man is his big or cat-like, kind eyes.

Pisces woman usually keeps up with the newest fashions, but she's never tacky. On the contrary, there's always a feminine allure to the typical Pisces woman.

What Attracts Pisces?

To attract a Pisces woman, a man must be a bit dapper but very tasteful. Loud, gaudy, or vulgar clothing (or speech) turns off a Pisces woman quicker than you can imagine. No jewelry, please! Pisces woman does not normally date men who wear chains or an earring. Pisces man likes a woman with a very clean, neat look. Little or no makeup is preferred, and long hair can be a big turn-on as long as it's back, up, or simply styled. Short hair is great, too. Though Pisces man likes sexy, he'll favor a more plainly dressed—conservative, casual, or even a bit funky if it's in an artsy way—woman for the long haul.

Pillow Talk: Signs in the Bedroom

Pisces tends to be secretive about her sex life. She's not apt to relate personal details to friends or acquaintances. But one thing is for sure: When the lights go out, she turns on! Pisces is sexy, sensual, and loving. Though she's less likely than most other signs to jump from bed to bed, it's not entirely against her principles if she feels something for the person in question (even if she doesn't plan on staying forever). However, emotionless sex for a Pisces is like being a fish out of water—especially for Pisces woman. She'll want to feel excited about you and the way things are going. That's when she'll let loose.

The Secret Pisces Man

Pisces man, like Pisces woman, always feels a bit above everyone else in the room. It's a smug sense of security he has, and it comes from his seemingly superior intelligence (not from self-assuredness of his looks). He may not brag, swagger, or put it out there, but Pisces man is always convinced that one could do much worse than to be with him. In fact, he'll be quite miffed if a woman picks another man over him. He's the first to secretly list the winner's faults. He may even tell you about them. But he'll never beg. Pisces man will never woo a woman by dropping to his knees.

Romance Counts

To seduce a Pisces man, be romantic. Open a bottle of wine, light some candles, and ask him to read you his poetry. Chances are good that he has something on hand, waiting.

 FACT

Pisces man is passionate and sensual. He wants to be respected and appreciated for his creativity and his sharp mind. If he intuits that you're the least bit superficial or flaky, he'll run the other way.

Don't compliment him excessively on his looks—if you do, make sure to also compliment him on his personality or character—he wants a connection of the mind. Talk about the future, the world, and things of nature and beauty. Stay away from gossiping about other people, which will make him not trust you, and talking too much about your future life together. Don't push too hard too fast.

The Secret Pisces Woman

Pisces woman is an ace at knowing just how to make the man of her choice fall head over heels in love. If she's not succeeding in doing this, she's simply with the wrong man—one who doesn't have strong feelings for her, perhaps. She has a way of operating, though, every time. Although she's nurturing and affectionate, she'll pull away to punish her man for something he's done. At this point, her mate has to make it up to her to win her back. The reason Pisces woman does this? It works. Most men respond to her very well, indeed.

She Wants to be Wooed and Courted

Seducing a Pisces woman is never as easy as just a good line, a handsome face, or an expensive dinner. Once again, it's the whole package. She loves to laugh and also to listen—she's a great listener. She doesn't necessarily need to hear words of love every five minutes, but she will expect it to come out in her partner's actions when he's with her.

He must be incredibly thoughtful and treat her like a real woman. Anything less will turn her cold. Though she tends to go for less gregarious types, she'll want an intelligent, adventurous man who will be exciting in bed, too. Earthy, exceptionally practical men turn her off and will not bring out her sultry, sensuous nature. In bed, Pisces woman can be persuaded to try almost anything—once. She does it out of curiosity and to appease the man she loves. Yes, Pisces woman is a gem. If she's treated like one, she won't stop at anything to treat her man like one, too.

Sun Love Matches

Pisces is a feeling sign, like all Water signs—and Fire signs as well. The whole myth "water puts out fire" is a gross misconception in the astrology world. Instead, Fire and Water are more alike than not. Fire stokes the Fire within Water and, together they balance each other. Both are passionate, emotionally sentimental, sweet in love, and sensitive—not very likely to think or rationalize things away (like some Air or Earth signs).

The only problem in the combination of Fire and Water signs is that Fire is more independent, while Water is usually more clingy (Cancer) or possessive (Scorpio). Pisces, though, is more balanced. He doesn't usually have the typical Water traits in excess. In fact, Pisces woman can be quite independent at times. Read on to learn about the matches for Pisces woman.

Pisces Man

This relationship can be made in heaven, or it just won't work. Together, Pisces woman and Pisces man can dream dreams, ponder the world, and intuit all things around them. Actually, they can instinctively feel each other and know what the other is thinking with astonishing accuracy. But criticism or wanting to do things "perfectly" could be an issue here. Pisces woman holds the reins. In bed, their relationship should be sensual and erotic. If Pisces man has some Fire in his chart, especially in his Venus or Mars, this could be a passionate, loving match. This is a very possible long-term thing and a possible marriage, too.

 ALERT!

> The Pisces-to-Pisces bond could even be a little frightening if both are not ready to accept something real in terms of marriage and long-term partnership.

Aries Man

With these two together, it seems anything is possible. Aries is the breath of fresh air Pisces woman has been waiting for. He forces her to look at the world through optimistic eyes. He brings out her spontaneity and her femininity. He makes her feel wanted and loved—at least in the beginning. If he's really serious about winning her and keeping her, he will. If he's not, she'll sense it. Pisces is actually good for an Aries man. She encourages him with the good stuff and holds him back from going off the deep end or acting too aggressively toward others. In bed, the two are complete fireworks. Aries opens up all kinds of possibilities for

Pisces, and she cherishes him for it. This can definitely be a long-term thing, with a good chance for marriage.

 ESSENTIAL

> Aries, the first sign of the zodiac, is like a child. Pisces is an old soul. Together, they balance each other out. Pisces woman is especially good for an Aries man. Strangely enough, however, Pisces man doesn't necessarily go with Aries woman.

Taurus Man

He's stubborn. She can be stubborn. Though he inspires her and can bring out her romantic side, there always seems to be something missing in the relationship. She respects him and he feels taken care of. He's found the nurturing, womanly soul he's been searching for. However, Pisces will not let Taurus get away with his temper tantrums, his sometimes childish antics, his possessive moods, or his spending/being stingy binges. Taurus may be able to keep her if he's a bit more evolved than the average customer. Also, these two tend to have two different senses of humor. In bed, sensual Taurus can be perfect for Pisces if there's some real affection there. Although this is not the ideal couple, it can also work. They're a long-term thing and a possible marriage.

Gemini Man

This is a difficult one. Gemini is a little self-conscious for Pisces' tastes. She wants someone a bit more direct and straightforward. Though he makes her laugh and they love to laugh at the world together, Gemini's affinity for gossiping about others can also turn Pisces woman off. When their relationship starts, it seems as if they can move mountains—and maybe they can. But Gemini's stop-go fickle tactics will irk Pisces to no uncertain degree: in other words, plenty.

 ESSENTIAL

> In truth, Pisces can be a bit refined for Gemini—and Gemini may even feel judged. But they also can seem every bit the perfect couple when they're out together.

In bed, Gemini knows exactly what to say to get Pisces going. It may even feel right, though Pisces will instinctively know they may not have a future together and this could freeze her up indefinitely. All in all, this is a possible long-term relationship, but it's not a probable marriage.

Cancer Man

It's funny how these two Water signs get along. Cancer actually confuses Pisces. She thinks she understands him, and then all of a sudden he's going off about how she's not trustworthy. She's annoyed by this part of him. He can get possessive with her. The strange thing is, sometimes she likes it, and sometimes it makes her want to escape. No matter—Cancer is determined to woo her. In fact, he inspires her to do great things. They both love security and family, and they make wonderful parents together. Though Cancer likes kinkiness in bed more than Pisces does, he can persuade her to do almost anything he wants. If Cancer lets Pisces control things out of bed to a large degree, this can really work. It's a very possible long-term thing and marriage.

Leo Man

Of the three Fire signs, Leo man is less "made for" Pisces woman. For starters, there's always a part of Pisces woman that Leo can't reach—and this makes him want her more. But he may get frustrated trying to dominate her, while Sagittarius and Aries will give up less easily. He wants it to be fiery, perfect love in the beginning and this is something he wants without effort.

 FACT

Though Pisces is wonderful at making Leo man feel every bit the powerful man he is, Leo sometimes feels that the compliments are forced (they aren't) and even, perhaps, that Pisces doesn't completely "get him."

Bed? All is fireworks and perfection. If both are willing to work at this relationship, and if Pisces doesn't get huffy with Leo when he criticizes her—making him feel guilty, which is not healthy for either of them—this can be a possible long-term relationship and maybe marriage as well.

Virgo Man

You know how they say opposites attract? Not in this case. Virgo may be far too wrapped up in business pursuits to give Pisces woman the kind of passionate relationship she dreams of. She wants romance and happily-ever-after. Virgo man may, in fact, love and adore her, but he has trouble expressing it. Also, making love could be difficult—to Pisces it may even feel like sexual gymnastics! He wants to change positions; she wants sensual variety. These two make good friends and even traveling partners, but marriage? A family? Maybe not. If Virgo has all Fire or Water, there's a chance. If not, this is not a likely long-term thing, and it's not a highly recommended marriage.

Libra Man

Feisty, charming Libra could seduce Pisces woman . . . but then what? His cool reserve draws Pisces in. She wants to discover all his mysteries. However, Libra can sometimes be a bit pessimistic for Pisces woman. Though she instinctively knows how to cheer him up, she's a bit disappointed with his self-pitying ways. This match can still feel like the real thing, though—and it may just be. Pisces and Libra need to give time to see where the relationship is going. This is not a probable long-term thing or marriage, but stranger things have happened.

Scorpio Man

Scorpio and Pisces are like cats in heat. The love-making is so perfect that if they ever make it out of the bed, they'll probably discover that they do, in fact, have much in common. Scorpio needs to open up to Pisces. Once he does, she'll feel more at ease. They can make each other laugh—in and out of bed.

 ALERT!

> When Pisces and Scorpio get together, though, watch out! Talk about the games people play. Both are sly and clever, and they instinctively know how to get the other to do and say what they want. In fact, guilt trips abound between Scorpio and Pisces!

Though Pisces may be a bit more refined than Scorpio man, their love for food and other sensuous pursuits go together extremely well. The only problem here is that Pisces will not let Scorpio manipulate her. He needs to feel in control, and she'll only let him feel that way if she decides to make it so. However, this can really work. They can have a probable long-term thing and a likely marriage.

Sagittarius Man

Strangely enough, if there's one man put on this earth for Pisces woman, it's Sagittarius man. They bring out the best in one another. Pisces woman does everything for the Archer. She makes him feel loved and protected, which is his ultimate desire with the right woman. She adores his macho, he-man ways. He excites her utterly. Pisces picks up the conversation when Sagittarius stops talking. She's a good listener. She respects Sagittarius's advice and gives him his due, and this makes him fall completely in love with her. He's also the adventurous, optimistic soul she's been searching for. This is an excellent chance for a long-term thing . . . marriage, too.

Capricorn Man

What is there to say about these two except that they probably have nothing in common? Spiritually and emotionally, they clash. Capricorn feels judged. He sees Pisces as a snob, a bit superficial and haughty for his tastes. He wants to be able to dress comfortably and casually when he feels like it. Pisces wants to spiff him up. Though he may comply, he'll resent her for it. He has a much more practical view of love, too, than idealistic Pisces. He may just burst her romantic bubble too many times. Bed, too, may be difficult—good for the short-term, but the passion could fade. This is not a probable long-term thing, and it's not a probable marriage, either.

Aquarius Man

Aquarius is the one sign that can really get Pisces into trouble. He inspires her to cook up mischief with him. In the beginning, they're like peas in a pod. Pisces loves Aquarius's way of looking at the world—he fascinates her. Strangely, she doesn't trust him. But maybe that's because he starts letting her down. If Pisces ever does feel in love with him, she won't for long if he behaves this way. Though Pisces is sexually attracted to Aquarius, the chemistry is stronger than the love. Therefore the sex is fantastic—it just gets better and better—while the relationship dwindles. This match is confusing at times, but there's a slight possibility it could work. All in all: not a probable long-term thing or marriage, but maybe—just maybe—if the heavens help out.

Love Planets: Venus and Mercury

Above all, remember that Pisces is the sign of the Sage. There's a born wisdom that comes with Pisces, always. Pisces in anyone's chart bestows sophistication, an air of conceit, and self-assuredness. Regardless of whether it's correct—which it usually is—Pisces trusts in intuition. Pisces in your chart will always make you a bit of a dreamer, or at least an optimist, depending on whether it falls in Venus or Mercury. Still, Pisces will enhance your goal-oriented nature, too. For Pisces woman (more than man), head-over-heels love isn't likely unless she's convinced that the person will be good for her.

Venus in Pisces

Once again, astrologers call Venus in Pisces "a dreamer, a romantic, an idealist." Along with Cancer, Pisces is one of the more starstruck of the signs—a person who lives for love. But Pisces, as opposed to other signs, wants real love—not *a* love. With Venus in Pisces, you want a partner to be your perfect match. That means best friend, lover, and everything to you. You also want him (or her) to feel the same way about you. Though you can be absolutely gaga in love, work and timing are also very important to you. Every element has to be right for you to go through with love . . . not just one component. Love must be integral and seemingly your destiny. You instinctively know the second you meet someone if you would be a good match together. Venus in Pisces goes with Venus in Cancer, Scorpio, Pisces, Sagittarius, Aries, and, perhaps, Leo.

Mercury in Pisces

You go for big ideas and big visions. Nothing about you is small. You excel in communicating. Your words are refined, beautiful, fluent, and can set the mood effortlessly. You're also wonderful at keeping the conversation going (though you don't ever talk just to fill space). Pensive you are, thoughtful and considerate. Though you don't mince words, you don't compliment just for the sake of it. You also tend to be politically diplomatic. Liars or those who shade the truth even a bit turn you off completely. Mercury in Pisces goes well with Mercury in Leo, Aries, Sagittarius, Aquarius, Scorpio, and Cancer.

☆ *Appendix A* ☆

Additional Resources

Ashman, Berne. *Sign Mates: An Astrological Guide to Love and Intimacy.* Llewellyn Publications: 2000.

Bartlett, Sarah. *Fated Attraction: Your Complete Zodiac Guide to Seduction.* HarperCollins: 2001.

Fenton, Sasha, and Jonathan Dee. *Moon Signs.* Collins & Brown Limited: 2001.

Golder, Carole. *Love Lives—Using Astrology to Build the Perfect Relationship with Any Star Sign.* Henry Holt and Company: 1989.

Holloway, Lee. *The Romantic Astrologer (A Guide to Love & Romance).* Andrews McMeel Publishing: 2000.

Keehn, Amy. *Love and War Between the Signs.* Prima Publishing: 1997.

Knight, Michele. *Good Sex (Starsigns).* MQ Publications Limited: 2002.

Lexander, Ren, and Geraldine Rose. *Seduction by the Stars: An Astrological Guide to Love, Lust, and Intimate Relationships.* Bantam Doubleday Dell Publishing Group, Inc.: 1995.

Macnaughton, Robin. *How to Seduce Any Man in the Zodiac.* HarperCollins: 1995.

Petulengro, Claire. *Love Stars.* Pan Macmillan Ltd.: 2001.

Pond, David. *Astrology & Relationships (Techniques for Harmonious Personal Connections).* Llewellyn Publications: 2001.

Rathgeb, Marlene Masini. *Sexual Astrology.* Avon Books, 1993.

West, John Anthony, and Jan Gerhard Toonder. *The Case for Astrology.* Penguin Books, Inc.: 1973.

Woolfolk, Joanna Martine. *The Only Astrology Book You'll Ever Need.* Madison Books: 2001.

Quick Sun Sign Chart

Sign	Dates	Gender	Element/ Quality
Aries, the Ram	3/21–4/19	M	Fire/ Cardinal
Taurus, the Bull	4/20–5/20	F	Earth/ Fixed
Gemini, the Twins	5/21–6/20	M	Air/ Mutable
Cancer, the Crab	6/21–7/22	F	Water/ Cardinal
Leo, the Lion	7/23–8/22	M	Fire/ Fixed
Virgo, the Virgin	8/23–9/22	F	Earth/ Mutable
Libra, the Scales	9/23–10/22	M	Air/ Cardinal
Scorpio, the Scorpion	10/23–11/21	F	Water/ Fixed
Sagittarius, the Archer	11/22–12/21	M	Fire/ Mutable
Capricorn, the Goat	12/22–1/19	F	Earth/ Cardinal
Aquarius, the Water Bearer	1/20–2/18	M	Air/ Fixed
Pisces, the Fish	2/19–3/20	F	Water/ Mutable

Extra: Cusp signs—that is, signs that share traits of neighboring signs—are those whose dates fall within two days of the cutoff mark. For example, someone born on February 18 or 19 is likely to have traits of Aquarius and Pisces, both.

☆ *Appendix C* ☆

Venus: Love Sign
Mercury: Communication and Intelligence

The sign in which Venus falls describes how you are as a romantic partner, spouse, or friend, as well as what you look for in a mate. Venus also indicates how you deal with love, whether you're nurturing and caring, possessive or trusting, idealistic, optimistic, or otherwise.

The sign in which Mercury falls, instead, describes how you communicate your ideas. It also shows how you express yourself (even in love), and how you gather and analyze information.

1950

Mercury			Venus		
Month	*Day*	*Sign*	*Month*	*Day*	*Sign*
JAN	1	AQU	JAN	1	AQU
JAN	15	CAP	APR	6	PIS
FEB	14	AQU	MAY	5	ARI
MAR	7	PIS	JUN	1	TAU
MAR	24	ARI	JUN	27	GEM
APR	8	TAU	JUL	22	CAN
JUN	14	GEM	AUG	16	LEO
JUL	2	CAN	SEP	10	VIR
JUL	16	LEO	OCT	4	LIB
AUG	2	VIR	OCT	28	SCO
AUG	27	LIB	NOV	21	SAG
SEP	10	VIR	DEC	14	CAP
OCT	9	LIB			
OCT	27	SCO			
NOV	15	SAG			
DEC	5	CAP			

1951

Mercury			Venus		
Month	*Day*	*Sign*	*Month*	*Day*	*Sign*
JAN	1	CAP	JAN	1	CAP
FEB	9	AQU	JAN	7	AQU
FEB	28	PIS	JAN	31	PIS
MAR	16	ARI	FEB	24	ARI
APR	2	TAU	MAR	21	TAU
MAY	1	ARI	APR	15	GEM
MAY	15	TAU	MAY	11	CAN
JUN	9	GEM	JUN	7	LEO
JUN	24	CAN	JUL	8	VIR
JUL	8	LEO	NOV	9	LIB
JUL	27	VIR	DEC	8	SCO
OCT	2	LIB			
OCT	19	SCO			
NOV	8	SAG			
DEC	1	CAP			
DEC	12	SAG			

1952

Mercury			Venus		
Month	Day	Sign	Month	Day	Sign
JAN	1	SAG	JAN	1	SCO
JAN	13	CAP	JAN	2	SAG
FEB	3	AQU	JAN	27	CAP
FEB	20	PIS	FEB	21	AQU
MAR	7	ARI	MAR	16	PIS
MAY	14	TAU	APR	9	ARI
MAY	31	GEM	MAY	4	TAU
JUN	14	CAN	MAY	28	GEM
JUN	30	LEO	JUN	22	CAN
SEP	7	VIR	JUL	16	LEO
SEP	23	LIB	AUG	9	VIR
OCT	11	SCO	SEP	3	LIB
NOV	1	SAG	SEP	27	SCO
			OCT	22	SAG
			NOV	15	CAP
			DEC	10	AQU

1953

Mercury			Venus		
Month	Day	Sign	Month	Day	Sign
JAN	1	SAG	JAN	1	AQU
JAN	6	CAP	JAN	5	PIS
JAN	25	AQU	FEB	2	ARI
FEB	11	PIS	MAR	14	TAU
MAR	2	ARI	MAR	31	ARI
MAR	15	PIS	JUN	5	TAU
APR	17	ARI	JUL	7	GEM
MAY	8	TAU	AUG	4	CAN
MAY	23	GEM	AUG	30	LEO
JUN	6	CAN	SEP	24	VIR
JUN	26	LEO	OCT	18	LIB
JUL	28	CAN	NOV	11	SCO
AUG	11	LEO	DEC	5	SAG
AUG	30	VIR	DEC	29	CAP
SEP	15	LIB			
OCT	4	SCO			
OCT	31	SAG			
NOV	6	SCO			
DEC	10	SAG			
DEC	30	CAP			

1954

Mercury			Venus		
Month	Day	Sign	Month	Day	Sign
JAN	1	CAP	JAN	1	CAP
JAN	18	AQU	JAN	22	AQU
FEB	4	PIS	FEB	15	PIS
APR	13	ARI	MAR	11	ARI
APR	30	TAU	APR	4	TAU
MAY	14	GEM	APR	28	GEM
MAY	30	CAN	MAY	23	CAN
AUG	7	LEO	JUN	17	LEO
AUG	22	VIR	JUL	13	VIR
SEP	8	LIB	AUG	9	LIB
SEP	29	SCO	SEP	6	SCO
NOV	4	LIB	OCT	23	SAG
NOV	11	SCO	OCT	27	SCO
DEC	4	SAG			
DEC	23	CAP			

1955

Mercury			Venus		
Month	Day	Sign	Month	Day	Sign
JAN	1	CAP	JAN	1	SCO
JAN	10	AQU	JAN	6	SAG
MAR	17	PIS	FEB	6	CAP
APR	6	ARI	MAR	4	AQU
APR	22	TAU	MAR	30	PIS
MAY	6	GEM	APR	24	ARI
JUL	13	CAN	MAY	19	TAU
JUL	30	LEO	JUN	13	GEM
AUG	14	VIR	JUL	8	CAN
SEP	1	LIB	AUG	1	LEO
NOV	8	SCO	AUG	25	VIR
NOV	27	SAG	SEP	18	LIB
DEC	16	CAP	OCT	13	SCO
			NOV	6	SAG
			NOV	30	CAP
			DEC	24	AQU

1956

Mercury			Venus		
Month	Day	Sign	Month	Day	Sign
JAN	1	CAP	JAN	1	AQU
JAN	4	AQU	JAN	17	PIS
FEB	2	CAP	FEB	11	ARI
FEB	15	AQU	MAR	7	TAU
MAR	11	PIS	APR	4	GEM
MAR	28	ARI	MAY	8	CAN
APR	12	TAU	JUN	23	GEM
APR	29	GEM	AUG	4	CAN
JUL	6	CAN	SEP	8	LEO
JUL	21	LEO	OCT	6	VIR
AUG	5	VIR	OCT	31	LIB
AUG	26	LIB	NOV	25	SCO
SEP	29	VIR	DEC	19	SAG
OCT	11	LIB			
OCT	31	SCO			
NOV	18	SAG			
DEC	8	CAP			

1957

Mercury			Venus		
Month	Day	Sign	Month	Day	Sign
JAN	1	CAP	JAN	1	SAG
FEB	12	AQU	JAN	12	CAP
MAR	4	PIS	FEB	5	AQU
MAR	20	ARI	MAR	1	PIS
APR	4	TAU	MAR	25	ARI
JUN	12	GEM	APR	19	TAU
JUN	28	CAN	MAY	13	GEM
JUL	12	LEO	JUN	6	CAN
JUL	30	VIR	JUL	1	LEO
OCT	6	LIB	JUL	26	VIR
OCT	23	SCO	AUG	20	LIB
NOV	11	SAG	SEP	14	SCO
DEC	2	CAP	OCT	10	SAG
DEC	28	SAG	NOV	5	CAP
			DEC	6	AQU

1958

Mercury			Venus		
Month	Day	Sign	Month	Day	Sign
JAN	1	SAG	JAN	1	AQU
JAN	14	CAP	APR	6	PIS
FEB	6	AQU	MAY	5	ARI
FEB	24	PIS	JUN	1	TAU
MAR	12	ARI	JUN	26	GEM
APR	2	TAU	JUL	22	CAN
APR	10	ARI	AUG	16	LEO
MAY	17	TAU	SEP	9	VIR
JUN	5	GEM	OCT	3	LIB
JUN	20	CAN	OCT	27	SCO
JUL	4	LEO	NOV	20	SAG
JUL	26	VIR	DEC	14	CAP
AUG	23	LEO			
SEP	11	VIR			
SEP	28	LIB			
OCT	16	SCO			
NOV	5	SAG			

1959

Mercury			Venus		
Month	Day	Sign	Month	Day	Sign
JAN	1	SAG	JAN	1	CAP
JAN	10	CAP	JAN	7	AQU
JAN	30	AQU	JAN	31	PIS
FEB	17	PIS	FEB	24	ARI
MAR	5	ARI	MAR	20	TAU
MAY	12	TAU	APR	14	GEM
MAY	28	GEM	MAY	10	CAN
JUN	11	CAN	JUN	6	LEO
JUN	28	LEO	JUL	8	VIR
SEP	5	VIR	SEP	20	LEO
OCT	21	LIB	SEP	25	VIR
OCT	9	SCO	NOV	9	LIB
OCT	31	SAG	DEC	7	SCO
NOV	25	SCO			
DEC	13	SAG			

1960

Mercury			Venus		
Month	Day	Sign	Month	Day	Sign
JAN	1	SAG	JAN	1	SCO
JAN	4	CAP	JAN	2	SAG
JAN	23	AQU	JAN	27	CAP
FEB	9	PIS	FEB	20	AQU
APR	16	ARI	MAR	16	PIS
MAY	4	TAU	APR	9	ARI
MAY	19	GEM	MAY	3	TAU
JUN	2	CAN	MAY	28	GEM
JUL	1	LEO	JUN	21	CAN
JUL	6	CAN	JUL	16	LEO
AUG	10	LEO	AUG	9	VIR
AUG	27	VIR	SEP	2	LIB
SEP	12	LIB	SEP	27	SCO
OCT	1	SCO	OCT	21	SAG
DEC	7	SAG	NOV	15	CAP
DEC	27	CAP	DEC	10	AQU

1961

Mercury			Venus		
Month	Day	Sign	Month	Day	Sign
JAN	1	CAP	JAN	1	AQU
JAN	14	AQU	JAN	5	PIS
FEB	1	PIS	FEB	2	ARI
FEB	24	AQU	JUN	5	TAU
MAR	18	PIS	JUL	7	GEM
APR	10	ARI	AUG	3	CAN
APR	26	TAU	AUG	29	LEO
MAY	10	GEM	SEP	23	VIR
MAY	28	CAN	OCT	18	LIB
AUG	4	LEO	NOV	11	SCO
AUG	18	VIR	DEC	5	SAG
SEP	4	LIB	DEC	29	CAP
SEP	27	SCO			
OCT	22	LIB			
NOV	10	SCO			
NOV	30	SAG			
DEC	20	CAP			

1962

Mercury			Venus		
Month	Day	Sign	Month	Day	Sign
JAN	1	CAP	JAN	1	CAP
JAN	7	AQU	JAN	21	AQU
MAR	15	PIS	FEB	14	PIS
APR	3	ARI	MAR	10	ARI
APR	18	TAU	APR	3	TAU
MAY	3	GEM	APR	28	GEM
JUL	11	CAN	MAY	23	CAN
JUL	26	LEO	JUN	17	LEO
AUG	10	VIR	JUL	12	VIR
AUG	29	LIB	AUG	8	LIB
NOV	5	SCO	SEP	7	SCO
NOV	23	SAG			
DEC	12	CAP			

1963

Mercury			Venus		
Month	Day	Sign	Month	Day	Sign
JAN	1	CAP	JAN	1	SCO
JAN	2	AQU	JAN	6	SAG
JAN	20	CAP	FEB	5	CAP
FEB	15	AQU	MAR	4	AQU
MAR	9	PIS	MAR	30	PIS
MAR	26	ARI	APR	24	ARI
APR	9	TAU	MAY	19	TAU
MAY	3	GEM	JUN	12	GEM
MAY	10	TAU	JUL	7	CAN
JUN	14	GEM	JUL	31	LEO
JUL	4	CAN	AUG	25	VIR
JUL	18	LEO	SEP	18	LIB
AUG	3	VIR	OCT	12	SCO
AUG	26	LIB	NOV	5	SAG
SEP	16	VIR	NOV	29	CAP
OCT	10	LIB	DEC	23	AQU
OCT	28	SCO			
NOV	16	SAG			
DEC	6	CAP			

1964

Mercury			Venus		
Month	*Day*	*Sign*	*Month*	*Day*	*Sign*
JAN	1	CAP	JAN	1	AQU
FEB	10	AQU	JAN	17	PIS
FEB	29	PIS	FEB	10	ARI
MAR	16	ARI	MAR	7	TAU
APR	2	TAU	APR	4	GEM
JUN	9	GEM	MAY	9	CAN
JUN	24	CAN	JUN	17	GEM
JUL	9	LEO	AUG	5	CAN
JUL	27	VIR	SEP	8	LEO
OCT	3	LIB	OCT	5	VIR
OCT	20	SCO	OCT	31	LIB
NOV	8	SAG	NOV	25	SCO
NOV	30	CAP	DEC	19	SAG
DEC	16	SAG			

1965

Mercury			Venus		
Month	*Day*	*Sign*	*Month*	*Day*	*Sign*
JAN	1	SAG	JAN	1	SAG
JAN	13	CAP	JAN	12	CAP
FEB	3	AQU	FEB	5	AQU
FEB	21	PIS	MAR	1	PIS
MAR	9	ARI	MAR	25	ARI
MAY	15	TAU	APR	18	TAU
JUN	2	GEM	MAY	12	GEM
JUN	16	CAN	JUN	6	CAN
JUL	1	LEO	JUN	30	LEO
JUL	31	VIR	JUL	25	VIR
AUG	3	LEO	AUG	19	LIB
SEP	8	VIR	SEP	13	SCO
SEP	25	LIB	OCT	9	SAG
OCT	12	SCO	NOV	5	CAP
NOV	2	SAG	DEC	7	AQU

1966

Mercury			Venus		
Month	Day	Sign	Month	Day	Sign
JAN	1	SAG	JAN	1	AQU
JAN	7	CAP	FEB	6	CAP
JAN	27	AQU	FEB	25	AQU
FEB	13	PIS	APR	6	PIS
MAR	3	ARI	MAY	5	ARI
MAR	22	PIS	MAY	31	TAU
APR	17	ARI	JUN	26	GEM
MAY	9	TAU	JUL	21	CAN
MAY	24	GEM	AUG	15	LEO
JUN	7	CAN	SEP	8	VIR
JUN	26	LEO	OCT	3	LIB
SEP	1	VIR	OCT	27	SCO
SEP	17	LIB	NOV	20	SAG
OCT	5	SCO	DEC	13	CAP
OCT	30	SAG			
NOV	13	SCO			
DEC	11	SAG			

1967

Mercury			Venus		
Month	Day	Sign	Month	Day	Sign
JAN	1	CAP	JAN	1	CAP
JAN	19	AQU	JAN	6	AQU
FEB	6	PIS	JAN	30	PIS
APR	14	ARI	FEB	23	ARI
MAY	1	TAU	MAR	20	TAU
MAY	16	GEM	APR	14	GEM
MAY	31	CAN	MAY	10	CAN
AUG	8	LEO	JUN	6	LEO
AUG	24	VIR	JUL	8	VIR
SEP	9	LIB	SEP	9	LEO
SEP	30	SCO	OCT	1	VIR
DEC	5	SAG	NOV	9	LIB
DEC	24	CAP	DEC	7	SCO

1968

	Mercury			Venus	
Month	Day	Sign	Month	Day	Sign
JAN	1	CAP	JAN	1	SAG
JAN	12	AQU	JAN	26	CAP
FEB	1	PIS	FEB	20	AQU
FEB	11	AQU	MAR	15	PIS
MAR	17	PIS	APR	8	ARI
APR	7	ARI	MAY	3	TAU
APR	22	TAU	MAY	27	GEM
MAY	6	GEM	JUN	21	CAN
MAY	29	CAN	JUL	15	LEO
JUN	13	GEM	AUG	8	VIR
JUL	13	CAN	SEP	2	LIB
JUL	31	LEO	SEP	26	SCO
AUG	15	VIR	OCT	21	SAG
SEP	1	LIB	NOV	14	CAP
SEP	28	SCO	DEC	9	AQU
OCT	7	LIB			
NOV	8	SCO			
NOV	27	SAG			
DEC	16	CAP			

1969

	Mercury			Venus	
Month	Day	Sign	Month	Day	Sign
JAN	1	CAP	JAN	1	AQU
JAN	4	AQU	JAN	4	PIS
MAR	12	PIS	FEB	2	ARI
MAR	30	ARI	JUN	6	TAU
APR	14	TAU	JUL	6	GEM
APR	30	GEM	AUG	3	CAN
JUL	8	CAN	AUG	29	LEO
JUL	22	LEO	SEP	23	VIR
AUG	7	VIR	OCT	17	LIB
AUG	27	LIB	NOV	10	SCO
OCT	7	VIR	DEC	4	SAG
OCT	9	LIB	DEC	28	CAP
NOV	1	SCO			
NOV	20	SAG			
DEC	9	CAP			

1970

Mercury			Venus		
Month	Day	Sign	Month	Day	Sign
JAN	1	CAP	JAN	1	CAP
JAN	4	AQU	JAN	21	AQU
JAN	4	CAP	FEB	14	PIS
FEB	13	AQU	MAR	10	ARI
MAR	5	PIS	APR	3	TAU
MAR	22	ARI	APR	27	GEM
APR	6	TAU	MAY	22	CAN
JUN	13	GEM	JUN	16	LEO
JUN	30	CAN	JUL	12	VIR
JUL	14	LEO	AUG	8	LIB
JUL	31	VIR	SEP	7	SCO
OCT	7	LIB			
OCT	25	SCO			
NOV	13	SAG			
DEC	3	CAP			

1971

Mercury			Venus		
Month	Day	Sign	Month	Day	Sign
JAN	1	CAP	JAN	1	SCO
JAN	2	SAG	JAN	7	SAG
JAN	14	CAP	FEB	5	CAP
FEB	7	AQU	MAR	4	AQU
FEB	26	PIS	MAR	29	PIS
MAR	14	ARI	APR	23	ARI
APR	1	TAU	MAY	18	TAU
APR	18	ARI	JUN	12	GEM
MAY	17	TAU	JUL	6	CAN
JUN	7	GEM	JUL	31	LEO
JUN	21	CAN	AUG	24	VIR
JUL	6	LEO	SEP	17	LIB
JUL	26	VIR	OCT	11	SCO
AUG	29	LEO	NOV	5	SAG
SEP	11	VIR	NOV	29	CAP
SEP	30	LIB	DEC	23	AQU
OCT	17	SCO			
NOV	6	SAG			

1972

Mercury			Venus		
Month	Day	Sign	Month	Day	Sign
JAN	1	SAG	JAN	1	AQU
JAN	11	CAP	JAN	16	PIS
JAN	31	AQU	FEB	10	ARI
FEB	18	PIS	MAR	7	TAU
MAR	5	ARI	APR	3	GEM
MAY	12	TAU	MAY	10	CAN
MAY	29	GEM	JUN	11	GEM
JUN	12	CAN	AUG	6	CAN
JUN	28	LEO	SEP	7	LEO
SEP	5	VIR	OCT	5	VIR
SEP	21	LIB	OCT	30	LIB
OCT	9	SCO	NOV	24	SCO
OCT	30	SAG	DEC	18	SAG
NOV	29	SCO			
DEC	12	SAG			

1973

Mercury			Venus		
Month	Day	Sign	Month	Day	Sign
JAN	1	SAG	JAN	1	SAG
JAN	4	CAP	JAN	11	CAP
JAN	23	AQU	FEB	4	AQU
FEB	9	PIS	FEB	28	PIS
APR	16	ARI	MAR	24	ARI
MAY	6	TAU	APR	18	TAU
MAY	20	GEM	MAY	12	GEM
JUN	4	CAN	JUN	5	CAN
JUN	27	LEO	JUN	30	LEO
JUL	16	CAN	JUL	25	VIR
AUG	11	LEO	AUG	19	LIB
AUG	28	VIR	SEP	13	SCO
SEP	13	LIB	OCT	9	SAG
OCT	2	SCO	NOV	5	CAP
DEC	8	SAG	DEC	7	AQU
DEC	28	CAP			

1974

Mercury			Venus		
Month	Day	Sign	Month	Day	Sign
JAN	1	CAP	JAN	1	AQU
JAN	16	AQU	JAN	29	CAP
FEB	2	PIS	FEB	28	AQU
MAR	2	AQU	APR	6	PIS
MAR	17	PIS	MAY	4	ARI
APR	11	ARI	MAY	31	TAU
APR	28	TAU	JUN	25	GEM
MAY	12	GEM	JUL	21	CAN
MAY	29	CAN	AUG	14	LEO
AUG	5	LEO	SEP	8	VIR
AUG	20	VIR	OCT	2	LIB
SEP	6	LIB	OCT	26	SCO
SEP	28	SCO	NOV	19	SAG
OCT	26	LIB	DEC	13	CAP
NOV	11	SCO			
DEC	2	SAG			
DEC	21	CAP			

1975

Mercury			Venus		
Month	Day	Sign	Month	Day	Sign
JAN	1	CAP	JAN	1	CAP
JAN	8	AQU	JAN	6	AQU
MAR	16	PIS	JAN	30	PIS
APR	4	ARI	FEB	23	ARI
APR	19	TAU	MAR	19	TAU
MAY	4	GEM	APR	13	GEM
JUL	12	CAN	MAY	9	CAN
JUL	28	LEO	JUN	6	LEO
AUG	12	VIR	JUL	9	VIR
AUG	30	LIB	SEP	2	LEO
NOV	6	SCO	OCT	4	VIR
NOV	25	SAG	NOV	9	LIB
DEC	14	CAP	DEC	7	SCO

1976

Mercury			Venus		
Month	*Day*	*Sign*	*Month*	*Day*	*Sign*
JAN	1	CAP	JAN	1	SAG
JAN	2	AQU	JAN	26	CAP
JAN	25	CAP	FEB	19	AQU
FEB	15	AQU	MAR	15	PIS
MAR	9	PIS	APR	8	ARI
MAR	26	ARI	MAY	2	TAU
APR	10	TAU	MAY	27	GEM
APR	29	GEM	JUN	20	CAN
MAY	19	TAU	JUL	14	LEO
JUN	13	GEM	AUG	8	VIR
JUL	4	CAN	SEP	1	LIB
JUL	18	LEO	SEP	26	SCO
AUG	3	VIR	OCT	20	SAG
AUG	25	LIB	NOV	14	CAP
SEP	21	VIR	DEC	9	AQU
OCT	10	LIB			
OCT	29	SCO			
NOV	16	SAG			
DEC	6	CAP			

1977

Mercury			Venus		
Month	*Day*	*Sign*	*Month*	*Day*	*Sign*
JAN	1	CAP	JAN	1	AQU
FEB	10	AQU	JAN	4	PIS
MAR	2	PIS	FEB	2	ARI
MAR	18	ARI	JUN	6	TAU
APR	3	TAU	JUL	6	GEM
JUN	10	GEM	AUG	2	CAN
JUN	26	CAN	AUG	28	LEO
JUL	10	LEO	SEP	22	VIR
JUL	28	VIR	OCT	17	LIB
OCT	4	LIB	NOV	10	SCO
OCT	21	SCO	DEC	4	SAG
NOV	9	SAG	DEC	27	CAP
DEC	1	CAP			
DEC	21	SAG			

1978

Mercury			Venus		
Month	Day	Sign	Month	Day	Sign
JAN	1	SAG	JAN	1	CAP
JAN	13	CAP	JAN	20	AQU
FEB	4	AQU	FEB	13	PIS
FEB	22	PIS	MAR	9	ARI
MAR	10	ARI	APR	2	TAU
MAY	16	TAU	APR	27	GEM
JUN	3	GEM	MAY	22	CAN
JUN	17	CAN	JUN	16	LEO
JUL	2	LEO	JUL	12	VIR
JUL	27	VIR	AUG	8	LIB
AUG	13	LEO	SEP	7	SCO
SEP	9	VIR			
SEP	26	LIB			
OCT	14	SCO			
NOV	3	SAG			

1979

Mercury			Venus		
Month	Day	Sign	Month	Day	Sign
JAN	1	SAG	JAN	1	SCO
JAN	8	CAP	JAN	7	SAG
JAN	28	AQU	FEB	5	CAP
FEB	14	PIS	MAR	3	AQU
MAR	3	ARI	MAR	29	PIS
MAR	28	PIS	APR	23	ARI
APR	17	ARI	MAY	18	TAU
MAY	10	TAU	JUN	11	GEM
MAY	26	GEM	JUL	6	CAN
JUN	9	CAN	JUL	30	LEO
JUN	27	LEO	AUG	24	VIR
SEP	2	VIR	SEP	17	LIB
SEP	18	LIB	OCT	11	SCO
OCT	7	SCO	NOV	4	SAG
OCT	30	SAG	NOV	28	CAP
NOV	18	SCO	DEC	22	AQU
DEC	12	SAG			

1980

Mercury			Venus		
Month	Day	Sign	Month	Day	Sign
JAN	1	SAG	JAN	1	AQU
JAN	2	CAP	JAN	16	PIS
JAN	21	AQU	FEB	9	ARI
FEB	7	PIS	MAR	6	TAU
APR	14	ARI	APR	3	GEM
MAY	2	TAU	MAY	12	CAN
MAY	16	GEM	JUN	5	GEM
MAY	31	CAN	AUG	6	CAN
AUG	9	LEO	SEP	7	LEO
AUG	24	VIR	OCT	4	VIR
SEP	10	LIB	OCT	30	LIB
SEP	30	SCO	NOV	24	SCO
DEC	5	SAG	DEC	18	SAG
DEC	25	CAP			

1981

Mercury			Venus		
Month	Day	Sign	Month	Day	Sign
JAN	1	CAP	JAN	1	SAG
JAN	12	AQU	JAN	11	CAP
JAN	31	PIS	FEB	4	AQU
FEB	16	AQU	FEB	28	PIS
MAR	18	PIS	MAR	24	ARI
APR	8	ARI	APR	17	TAU
APR	24	TAU	MAY	11	GEM
MAY	8	GEM	JUN	5	CAN
MAY	28	CAN	JUN	29	LEO
JUN	22	GEM	JUL	24	VIR
JUL	12	CAN	AUG	18	LIB
AUG	1	LEO	SEP	12	SCO
AUG	16	VIR	OCT	9	SAG
SEP	2	LIB	NOV	5	CAP
SEP	27	SCO	DEC	8	AQU
OCT	14	LIB			
NOV	9	SCO			
NOV	28	SAG			
DEC	17	CAP			

1982

Mercury			Venus		
Month	Day	Sign	Month	Day	Sign
JAN	1	CAP	JAN	1	AQU
JAN	5	AQU	JAN	23	CAP
MAR	13	PIS	MAR	2	AQU
MAR	31	ARI	APR	6	PIS
APR	15	TAU	MAY	4	ARI
MAY	1	GEM	MAY	30	TAU
JUL	9	CAN	JUN	25	GEM
JUL	24	LEO	JUL	20	CAN
AUG	8	VIR	AUG	14	LEO
AUG	28	LIB	SEP	7	VIR
NOV	3	SCO	OCT	2	LIB
NOV	21	SAG	OCT	26	SCO
DEC	10	CAP	NOV	18	SAG
			DEC	12	CAP

1983

Mercury			Venus		
Month	Day	Sign	Month	Day	Sign
JAN	1	AQU	JAN	1	CAP
JAN	12	CAP	JAN	5	AQU
FEB	14	AQU	JAN	29	PIS
MAR	7	PIS	FEB	22	ARI
MAR	23	ARI	MAR	19	TAU
APR	7	TAU	APR	13	GEM
JUN	14	GEM	MAY	9	CAN
JUL	1	CAN	JUN	6	LEO
JUL	15	LEO	JUL	10	VIR
AUG	1	VIR	AUG	27	LEO
AUG	29	LIB	OCT	5	VIR
SEP	6	VIR	NOV	9	LIB
OCT	8	LIB	DEC	6	SCO
OCT	26	SCO			
NOV	14	SAG			
DEC	4	CAP			

1984

Mercury			Venus		
Month	Day	Sign	Month	Day	Sign
JAN	1	CAP	JAN	1	SAG
FEB	9	AQU	JAN	25	CAP
FEB	27	PIS	FEB	19	AQU
MAR	14	ARI	MAR	14	PIS
MAR	31	TAU	APR	7	ARI
APR	25	ARI	MAY	2	TAU
MAY	15	TAU	MAY	26	GEM
JUN	7	GEM	JUN	20	CAN
JUN	22	CAN	JUL	14	LEO
JUL	6	LEO	AUG	7	VIR
JUL	26	VIR	SEP	1	LIB
SEP	30	LIB	SEP	25	SCO
OCT	18	SCO	OCT	20	SAG
NOV	6	SAG	NOV	13	CAP
DEC	1	CAP	DEC	9	AQU
DEC	7	SAG			

1985

Mercury			Venus		
Month	Day	Sign	Month	Day	Sign
JAN	1	SAG	JAN	1	AQU
JAN	11	CAP	JAN	4	PIS
FEB	1	AQU	FEB	2	ARI
FEB	18	PIS	JUN	6	TAU
MAR	7	ARI	JUL	6	GEM
MAY	14	TAU	AUG	2	CAN
MAY	30	GEM	AUG	28	LEO
JUN	13	CAN	SEP	22	VIR
JUN	29	LEO	OCT	16	LIB
SEP	6	VIR	NOV	9	SCO
SEP	22	LIB	DEC	3	SAG
OCT	10	SCO	DEC	27	CAP
OCT	31	SAG			
DEC	4	SCO			
DEC	12	SAG			

1986

Mercury			Venus		
Month	Day	Sign	Month	Day	Sign
JAN	1	SAG	JAN	1	CAP
JAN	5	CAP	JAN	20	AQU
JAN	25	AQU	FEB	13	PIS
FEB	11	PIS	MAR	9	ARI
MAR	3	ARI	APR	2	TAU
MAR	11	PIS	APR	26	GEM
APR	17	ARI	MAY	21	CAN
MAY	7	TAU	JUN	15	LEO
MAY	22	GEM	JUL	11	VIR
JUN	5	CAN	AUG	7	LIB
JUN	26	LEO	SEP	7	SCO
JUL	23	CAN			
AUG	11	LEO			
AUG	30	VIR			
SEP	15	LIB			
OCT	4	SCO			
DEC	10	SAG			
DEC	29	CAP			

1987

Mercury			Venus		
Month	Day	Sign	Month	Day	Sign
JAN	1	CAP	JAN	1	SCO
JAN	17	AQU	JAN	7	SAG
FEB	4	PIS	FEB	5	CAP
MAR	11	AQU	MAR	3	AQU
MAR	13	PIS	MAR	28	PIS
APR	12	ARI	APR	22	ARI
APR	29	TAU	MAY	17	TAU
MAY	13	GEM	JUN	11	GEM
MAY	30	CAN	JUL	5	CAN
AUG	6	LEO	JUL	30	LEO
AUG	21	VIR	AUG	23	VIR
SEP	7	LIB	SEP	16	LIB
SEP	28	SCO	OCT	10	SCO
NOV	1	LIB	NOV	3	SAG
NOV	11	SCO	NOV	28	CAP
DEC	3	SAG	DEC	22	AQU
DEC	22	CAP			

1988

	Mercury			Venus	
Month	Day	Sign	Month	Day	Sign
JAN	1	CAP	JAN	1	AQU
JAN	10	AQU	JAN	15	PIS
MAR	16	PIS	FEB	9	ARI
APR	4	ARI	MAR	6	TAU
APR	20	TAU	APR	3	GEM
MAY	4	GEM	MAY	17	CAN
JUL	12	CAN	MAY	27	GEM
JUL	28	LEO	AUG	6	CAN
AUG	12	VIR	SEP	7	LEO
AUG	30	LIB	OCT	4	VIR
NOV	6	SCO	OCT	29	LIB
NOV	25	SAG	NOV	23	SCO
DEC	14	CAP	DEC	17	SAG

1989

	Mercury			Venus	
Month	Day	Sign	Month	Day	Sign
JAN	1	CAP	JAN	1	SAG
JAN	2	AQU	JAN	10	CAP
JAN	29	CAP	FEB	3	AQU
FEB	14	AQU	FEB	27	PIS
MAR	10	PIS	MAR	23	ARI
MAR	28	ARI	APR	16	TAU
APR	11	TAU	MAY	11	GEM
APR	29	GEM	JUN	4	CAN
MAY	28	TAU	JUN	29	LEO
JUN	12	GEM	JUL	24	VIR
JUL	6	CAN	AUG	18	LIB
JUL	20	LEO	SEP	12	SCO
AUG	5	VIR	OCT	8	SAG
AUG	26	LIB	NOV	5	CAP
SEP	26	VIR	DEC	10	AQU
OCT	11	LIB			
OCT	30	SCO			
NOV	18	SAG			
DEC	7	CAP			

1990

Mercury			Venus		
Month	Day	Sign	Month	Day	Sign
JAN	1	CAP	JAN	1	AQU
FEB	12	AQU	JAN	16	CAP
MAR	3	PIS	MAR	3	AQU
MAR	20	ARI	APR	6	PIS
APR	4	TAU	MAY	4	ARI
JUN	12	GEM	MAY	30	TAU
JUN	27	CAN	JUN	25	GEM
JUL	11	LEO	JUL	20	CAN
JUL	29	VIR	AUG	13	LEO
OCT	5	LIB	SEP	7	VIR
OCT	23	SCO	OCT	1	LIB
NOV	11	SAG	OCT	25	SCO
DEC	2	CAP	NOV	18	SAG
DEC	25	SAG	DEC	12	CAP

Index

A

Aquarius, 207–224
    Aquarius and, 215–216
    Aries and, 23–24, 216–217
    Cancer and, 86, 219
    Capricorn and, 198–199,
        222–223
    Gemini and, 66–67, 218–219
    Leo and, 105–106, 220
    Libra and, 140–141, 221
    Pisces and, 216, 241
    Sagittarius and, 177–178, 222
    Scorpio and, 159, 221–222
    Taurus and, 45–46, 217–218
    Virgo and, 122–123, 220
Aries, 1–26
    Aquarius and, 23–24,
        216–217
    Aries and, 16
    Cancer and, 18–19, 87
    Capricorn and, 22–23,
        199–200
    Gemini and, 17–18, 67–68
    Leo and, 19–20, 107
    Libra and, 20–21, 141–142
    Pisces and, 24, 234–235
    Sagittarius and, 22, 179
    Scorpio and, 21–22, 160
    Taurus and, 17, 46–47
    Virgo and, 20, 124

C

Cancer, 71–90
    Aquarius and, 86, 219
    Aries and, 18–19, 87
    Cancer and, 81
    Capricorn and, 85–86, 201
    Gemini and, 62, 88–89
    Leo and, 81–82, 109
    Libra and, 83–84, 143
    Pisces and, 86–87,
        236–237
    Sagittarius and, 84–85,
        180–181
    Scorpio and, 84, 161–162
    Taurus and, 41–42, 88
    Virgo and, 82–83, 126
Capricorn, 187–206
    Aquarius and, 198–199,
        222–223
    Aries and, 22–23, 199–200
    Cancer and, 85–86, 201
    Capricorn and, 197–198
    Gemini and, 66, 200–201
    Leo and, 105, 202
    Libra and, 140, 203
    Pisces and, 199, 240
    Sagittarius and, 177,
        204–205
    Scorpio and, 158–159,
        203–204
    Taurus and, 45, 200
    Virgo and, 122, 202–203

G

Gemini, 49–70
    Aquarius and, 66–67,
        218–219
    Aries and, 17–18, 67–68
    Cancer and, 62, 88–89

Gemini—*continued*
    Capricorn and, 66, 200–201
    Gemini and, 61–62
    Leo and, 62–63, 108
    Libra and, 64, 142–143
    Pisces and, 67, 236
    Sagittarius and, 65, 180
    Scorpio and, 65, 161
    Taurus and, 41, 68
    Virgo and, 63–64, 125

L
Leo, 91–110
    Aquarius and, 105–106, 220
    Aries and, 19–20, 107
    Cancer and, 81–82, 109
    Capricorn and, 105, 202
    Gemini and, 62–63, 108
    Leo and, 101–102
    Libra and, 102–103, 143–144
    Pisces and, 106–107,
        237–238
    Sagittarius and, 104,
        181–182
    Scorpio and, 103–104,
        162–163
    Taurus and, 42, 107–108
    Virgo and, 102, 126–127
Libra, 129–146
    Aquarius and, 140–141, 221
    Aries and, 20–21, 141–142
    Cancer and, 83–84, 143
    Capricorn and, 140, 203
    Gemini and, 64, 142–143
    Leo and, 102–103, 143–144
    Libra and, 138–139
    Pisces and, 141, 238–239
    Sagittarius and, 139–140,
        182–183

    Scorpio and, 139, 163–164
    Taurus and, 43, 142
    Virgo and, 120, 144

M
Mercury, 245–266
    in Aquarius, 224
    in Aries, 25–26
    in Cancer, 90
    in Capricorn, 206
    in Gemini, 70
    in Leo, 110
    in Libra, 145–146
    in Pisces, 242
    in Sagittarius, 185
    in Scorpio, 165
    in Taurus, 48
    in Virgo, 128

P
Pisces, 225–242
    Aquarius and, 216, 241
    Aries and, 24, 234–235
    Cancer and, 86–87, 236–237
    Capricorn and, 199, 240
    Gemini and, 67, 236
    Leo and, 106–107, 237–238
    Libra and, 141, 238–239
    Pisces and, 233–234
    Sagittarius and, 178–179,
        240
    Scorpio and, 159–160, 239
    Taurus and, 46, 235
    Virgo and, 123–124, 238

S
Sagittarius, 167–185
    Aquarius and, 177–178, 222
    Aries and, 22, 179

Cancer and, 84–85, 180–181
Capricorn and, 177,
    204–205
Gemini and, 65, 180
Leo and, 104, 181–182
Libra and, 139–140, 182–183
Pisces and, 178–179, 240
Sagittarius and, 176–177
Scorpio and, 158, 183
Taurus and, 44–45, 179–180
Virgo and, 121–122, 182
Scorpio, 147–165
    Aquarius and, 159, 221–222
    Aries and, 21–22, 160
    Cancer and, 84, 161–162
    Capricorn and, 158–159,
        203–204
    Gemini and, 65, 161
    Leo and, 103–104, 162–163
    Libra and, 139, 163–164
    Pisces and, 159–160, 239
    Sagittarius and, 158, 183
    Scorpio and, 157
    Taurus and, 44, 160–161
    Virgo and, 120–121, 163

T
Taurus, 27–48
    Aquarius and, 45–46,
        217–218
    Aries and, 17, 46–47
    Cancer and, 41–42, 88
    Capricorn and, 45, 200
    Gemini and, 41, 68
    Leo and, 42, 107–108
    Libra and, 43, 142
    Pisces and, 46, 235
    Sagittarius and, 44–45,
        179–180

Scorpio and, 44, 160–161
Taurus and, 40–41
Virgo and, 43, 124–125

V
Venus, 245–266
    in Aquarius, 224
    in Aries, 25
    in Cancer, 90
    in Capricorn, 205
    in Gemini, 69–70
    in Leo, 110
    in Libra, 145
    in Pisces, 242
    in Sagittarius, 184–185
    in Scorpio, 164–165
    in Taurus, 48
    in Virgo, 127–128
Virgo, 111–128
    Aquarius and, 122–123, 220
    Aries and, 20, 124
    Cancer and, 82–83, 126
    Capricorn and, 122,
        202–203
    Gemini and, 63–64, 125
    Leo and, 102, 126–127
    Libra and, 120, 144
    Pisces and, 123–124, 238
    Sagittarius and, 121–122,
        182
    Scorpio and, 120–121, 163
    Taurus and, 43, 124–125
    Virgo and, 119–120

Z
zodiac chart, 244

We Have EVERYTHING!

BUSINESS

Everything® **Business Planning Book**
Everything® **Coaching and Mentoring Book**
Everything® **Fundraising Book**
Everything® **Home-Based Business Book**
Everything® **Leadership Book**
Everything® **Managing People Book**
Everything® **Network Marketing Book**
Everything® **Online Business Book**
Everything® **Project Management Book**
Everything® **Selling Book**
Everything® **Start Your Own Business Book**
Everything® **Time Management Book**

COMPUTERS

Everything® **Build Your Own Home Page Book**
Everything® **Computer Book**
Everything® **Internet Book**
Everything® **Microsoft® Word 2000 Book**

COOKBOOKS

Everything® **Barbecue Cookbook**
Everything® **Bartender's Book, $9.95**
Everything® **Chinese Cookbook**
Everything® **Chocolate Cookbook**
Everything® **Cookbook**
Everything® **Dessert Cookbook**
Everything® **Diabetes Cookbook**
Everything® **Low-Carb Cookbook**
Everything® **Low-Fat High-Flavor Cookbook**

Everything® **Mediterranean Cookbook**
Everything® **Mexican Cookbook**
Everything® **One-Pot Cookbook**
Everything® **Pasta Book**
Everything® **Quick Meals Cookbook**
Everything® **Slow Cooker Cookbook**
Everything® **Soup Cookbook**
Everything® **Thai Cookbook**
Everything® **Vegetarian Cookbook**
Everything® **Wine Book**

HEALTH

Everything® **Anti-Aging Book**
Everything® **Diabetes Book**
Everything® **Dieting Book**
Everything® **Herbal Remedies Book**
Everything® **Hypnosis Book**
Everything® **Menopause Book**
Everything® **Nutrition Book**
Everything® **Reflexology Book**
Everything® **Stress Management Book**
Everything® **Vitamins, Minerals, and Nutritional Supplements Book**

HISTORY

Everything® **American History Book**
Everything® **Civil War Book**
Everything® **Irish History & Heritage Book**
Everything® **Mafia Book**
Everything® **World War II Book**

HOBBIES & GAMES

Everything® **Bridge Book**
Everything® **Candlemaking Book**
Everything® **Casino Gambling Book**

Everything® **Chess Basics Book**
Everything® **Collectibles Book**
Everything® **Crossword and Puzzle Book**
Everything® **Digital Photography Book**
Everything® **Family Tree Book**
Everything® **Games Book**
Everything® **Knitting Book**
Everything® **Magic Book**
Everything® **Motorcycle Book**
Everything® **Online Genealogy Book**
Everything® **Photography Book**
Everything® **Pool & Billiards Book**
Everything® **Quilting Book**
Everything® **Scrapbooking Book**
Everything® **Soapmaking Book**

HOME IMPROVEMENT

Everything® **Feng Shui Book**
Everything® **Gardening Book**
Everything® **Home Decorating Book**
Everything® **Landscaping Book**
Everything® **Lawn Care Book**
Everything® **Organize Your Home Book**

KIDS' STORY BOOKS

Everything® **Bedtime Story Book**
Everything® **Bible Stories Book**
Everything® **Fairy Tales Book**
Everything® **Mother Goose Book**

LANGUAGE

Everything® **Learning French Book**

Everything® **Learning German Book**
Everything® **Learning Italian Book**
Everything® **Learning Latin Book**
Everything® **Learning Spanish Book**
Everything® **Sign Language Book**

MUSIC

Everything® **Drums Book (with CD), $19.95 ($31.95 CAN)**
Everything® **Guitar Book**
Everything® **Playing Piano and Keyboards Book**
Everything® **Rock & Blues Guitar Book (with CD), $19.95 ($31.95 CAN)**
Everything® **Songwriting Book**

NEW AGE

Everything® **Astrology Book**
Everything® **Divining the Future Book**
Everything® **Dreams Book**
Everything® **Ghost Book**
Everything® **Meditation Book**
Everything® **Numerology Book**
Everything® **Palmistry Book**
Everything® **Psychic Book**
Everything® **Spells & Charms Book**
Everything® **Tarot Book**
Everything® **Wicca and Witchcraft Book**

PARENTING

Everything® **Baby Names Book**
Everything® **Baby Shower Book**
Everything® **Baby's First Food Book**
Everything® **Baby's First Year Book**
Everything® **Breastfeeding Book**
Everything® **Father-to-Be Book**

Everything® **Get Ready for Baby Book**
Everything® **Home-schooling Book**
Everything® **Parent's Guide to Positive Discipline**
Everything® **Potty Training Book, $9.95 ($15.95 CAN)**
Everything® **Pregnancy Book, 2nd Ed.**
Everything® **Pregnancy Fitness Book**
Everything® **Pregnancy Organizer, $15.00 ($22.95 CAN)**
Everything® **Toddler Book**
Everything® **Tween Book**

PERSONAL FINANCE

Everything® **Budgeting Book**
Everything® **Get Out of Debt Book**
Everything® **Get Rich Book**
Everything® **Homebuying Book, 2nd Ed.**
Everything® **Homeselling Book**
Everything® **Investing Book**
Everything® **Money Book**
Everything® **Mutual Funds Book**
Everything® **Online Investing Book**
Everything® **Personal Finance Book**
Everything® **Personal Finance in Your 20s & 30s Book**
Everything® **Wills & Estate Planning Book**

PETS

Everything® **Cat Book**
Everything® **Dog Book**
Everything® **Dog Training and Tricks Book**
Everything® **Horse Book**
Everything® **Puppy Book**
Everything® **Tropical Fish Book**

REFERENCE

Everything® **Astronomy Book**

Everything® **Car Care Book**
Everything® **Christmas Book, $15.00 ($21.95 CAN)**
Everything® **Classical Mythology Book**
Everything® **Einstein Book**
Everything® **Etiquette Book**
Everything® **Great Thinkers Book**
Everything® **Philosophy Book**
Everything® **Shakespeare Book**
Everything® **Tall Tales, Legends, & Other Outrageous Lies Book**
Everything® **Toasts Book**
Everything® **Trivia Book**
Everything® **Weather Book**

RELIGION

Everything® **Angels Book**
Everything® **Buddhism Book**
Everything® **Catholicism Book**
Everything® **Jewish History & Heritage Book**
Everything® **Judaism Book**
Everything® **Prayer Book**
Everything® **Saints Book**
Everything® **Understanding Islam Book**
Everything® **World's Religions Book**
Everything® **Zen Book**

SCHOOL & CAREERS

Everything® **After College Book**
Everything® **College Survival Book**
Everything® **Cover Letter Book**
Everything® **Get-a-Job Book**
Everything® **Hot Careers Book**
Everything® **Job Interview Book**
Everything® **Online Job Search Book**
Everything® **Resume Book, 2nd Ed.**
Everything® **Study Book**

SELF-HELP

Everything® **Dating Book**
Everything® **Divorce Book**
Everything® **Great Marriage Book**
Everything® **Great Sex Book**
Everything® **Romance Book**
Everything® **Self-Esteem Book**
Everything® **Success Book**

SPORTS & FITNESS

Everything® **Bicycle Book**
Everything® **Body Shaping Book**
Everything® **Fishing Book**
Everything® **Fly-Fishing Book**
Everything® **Golf Book**
Everything® **Golf Instruction Book**
Everything® **Pilates Book**
Everything® **Running Book**
Everything® **Sailing Book, 2nd Ed.**
Everything® **T'ai Chi and QiGong Book**
Everything® **Total Fitness Book**
Everything® **Weight Training Book**
Everything® **Yoga Book**

TRAVEL

Everything® **Guide to Las Vegas**
Everything® **Guide to New England**
Everything® **Guide to New York City**
Everything® **Guide to Washington D.C.**
Everything® **Travel Guide to The Disneyland Resort®, California Adventure®, Universal Studios®, and the Anaheim Area**

Everything® **Travel Guide to the Walt Disney World Resort®, Universal Studios®, and Greater Orlando, 3rd Ed.**

WEDDINGS

Everything® **Bachelorette Party Book**
Everything® **Bridesmaid Book**
Everything® **Creative Wedding Ideas Book**
Everything® **Jewish Wedding Book**
Everything® **Wedding Book, 2nd.Ed.**
Everything® **Wedding Checklist, $7.95 ($11.95 CAN)**
Everything® **Wedding Etiquette Book, $7.95 ($11.95 CAN)**
Everything® **Wedding Organizer, $15.00 ($22.95 CAN)**
Everything® **Wedding Shower Book, $7.95 ($12.95 CAN)**
Everything® **Wedding Vows Book, $7.95 ($11.95 CAN)**
Everything® **Weddings on a Budget Book, $9.95 ($15.95 CAN)**

WRITING

Everything® **Creative Writing Book**
Everything® **Get Published Book**
Everything® **Grammar and Style Book**
Everything® **Grant Writing Book**

Everything® **Guide to Writing Children's Books**
Everything® **Screenwriting Book**
Everything® **Writing Well Book**

EVERYTHING® KIDS' BOOKS

All titles are $6.95 and $10.95 CAN (unless otherwise noted)

Everything® **Kids' Baseball Book, 2nd Ed.**
Everything® **Kids' Bugs Book**
Everything® **Kids' Christmas Puzzle & Activity Book**
Everything® **Kids' Cookbook**
Everything® **Kids' Halloween Puzzle & Activity Book**
Everything® **Kids' Joke Book**
Everything® **Kids' Math Puzzles Book**
Everything® **Kids' Mazes Book**
Everything® **Kids' Money Book ($11.95 CAN)**
Everything® **Kids' Monsters Book**
Everything® **Kids' Nature Book ($11.95 CAN)**
Everything® **Kids' Puzzle Book**
Everything® **Kids' Science Experiments Book**
Everything® **Kids' Soccer Book**
Everything® **Kids' Travel Activity Book**

All Everything® books are priced at $12.95 or $14.95, unless otherwise stated.
Prices subject to change without notice.
Canadian prices range from $11.95–$31.95, and are subject to change without notice.

Available wherever books are sold!
To order, call 1-800-872-5627 or visit everything.com
Everything® and everything.com® are registered trademarks of F+W Publications, Inc.